O B J E C T

D1577935

A book series about the hidden lives of ordinary things.

Series Editors:

Ian Bogost and Christopher Schaberg

Advisory Board:

Sara Ahmed, Jane Bennett, Johanna Drucker, Raiford Guins, Graham Harman, renée hoogland, Pam Houston, Eileen Joy, Douglas Kahn, Daniel Miller, Esther Milne, Timothy Morton, Nigel Thrift, Kathleen Stewart, Rob Walker, Michele White.

In association with

 Georgia | **Center for**
Tech | **Media Studies**

BOOKS IN THE SERIES

silence

JOHN BIGUENET

Bloomsbury Academic
An imprint of Bloomsbury Publishing Inc

B L O O M S B U R Y
NEW YORK · LONDON · OXFORD · NEW DELHI · SYDNEY

Bloomsbury Academic

An imprint of Bloomsbury Publishing Inc

1385 Broadway	50 Bedford Square
New York	London
NY 10018	WC1B 3DP
USA	UK

www.bloomsbury.com

**BLOOMSBURY and the Diana logo are trademarks of
Bloomsbury Publishing Plc**

First published 2015

© John Biguenet, 2015

Library of Congress Cataloging-in-Publication Data
A catalog record for this book is available from the Library of Congress.

ISBN: PB: 978-1-6289-2142-7
ePub: 978-1-6289-2144-1
ePDF: 978-1-6289-2146-5

Series: Object Lessons

Typeset by Deanta Global Publishing Services, Chennai, India
Printed and bound in the United States of America

for Sha

"*The rest is silence.*"

—WILLIAM SHAKESPEARE

CONTENTS

I

1 WHAT IS SILENCE?

We may conjecture that somewhere in the cosmos, beyond the border of all human trace, a zone of silence awaits (always receding, of course, before the advance of future explorers), a great sea of stillness unperturbed by the animate, an utterly quiet virgin territory. But our imagination misleads us if we conceive of silence as a destination at which we might arrive.

Similarly, in a less poetic vein, if we assume that silence is merely the absence of sound waves or, more precisely, the absence of a medium capable of transmitting sound waves, though we are correct, we miss a larger point: silence is a measure of human limitation. Beyond the boundaries of the upper and lower ranges of the ear's capacity to sense sound lies the subject of this book, and therefore it is necessarily something we will never physically experience. For silence, after all, is a term we reserve for that which we cannot perceive, the inaudible. (Of course, if we cannot hear silence, what is it that the deaf experience?)

The implications of this argument are easier to grasp if we turn to sight and the organ analogous to the ear, the eye. We have grown quite comfortable with the modern unraveling of the distinction between the visible and the invisible. Just as we believe in the existence of a silent reality—in the efficacy of a dog whistle, for example, inaudibly screeching its signal to a floppy-eared pet—we accept the existence of hadrons and the quarks of which they are constituted. Our scientists have persuaded us that phenomena invisible to our eyes because of optical limitation do, in fact, exist. They confirm that existence through indirect observations, often ingenious in conception.

So the misplaced faith we once expressed in such common-sense formulas as "Seeing is believing" yields to a modern belief in things unseen—a world beyond the senses. We do not dispute, for example, the underlying fabric of matter—woven of invisible protons, neutrons, and electrons, we believe, but utterly fantastic without the mathematics to support our belief.

And this extension of the natural world to incorporate the unseen and the unheard proliferates even as modernity wars relentlessly against other forms of invisibility and inaudibility, now routinely dismissed as the supernatural. We are expected to acknowledge the existence of radiation pulsing from the center of our galaxy that we neither see nor hear but nonetheless measure with a radio telescope, a device whose very name suggests the unity of the reality unperceived by our eyes or ears. At the same time, growing popular opinion regards necromancers as charlatans and belief in ghosts as symptomatic of psychological affliction.

All this is no doubt easy to accept until one attempts to distinguish the unseen and unheard we ridicule from that which we worship. For example, what sets apart the adepts of the occult from the clergy of established religions? If we press further into this dilemma, we may well ask whether Jeanne d'Arc, a saint listed in the *Martyrology* of the Catholic Church, responded to heavenly voices or whether she suffered from auditory hallucinations, commonly associated by mental health experts today with schizophrenia and psychosis?

It would, of course, be presumptuous to answer for the reader such questions. But it is difficult to dispute our current readiness to concede the reality of a universe of unheard and unseen phenomena discovered in only the last few hundred years while debating (and increasingly rejecting) the existence of other phenomena also beyond the scope of our senses, and yet nearly universally accepted for millennia.

A Harris Poll, conducted in late 2013, found belief in God, for example, had fallen from 82 percent to 75 percent among US adults in just four years, with similar declines in belief in miracles, heaven, and the afterlife of the soul, angels and devils, and witches.[1] If more concrete evidence is wanted, *The Wall Street Journal* noted in a 2015 article that Dutch ecclesiastical authorities anticipate shuttering nearly 1,100 of the country's 1,600 Catholic churches in the next decade and 700 Protestant churches within the next four years. Germany has closed 515 churches in the past decade, while 200 Danish churches are viewed as unsustainable.[2]

On the one hand, we have learned to surpass our senses, discovering what had been beyond our ken. On the other hand, as a result of our success in devising protocols to verify that knowledge, we grow skeptical of belief in the imperceptible that resists our methods of confirmation.

So though an object with which most of us feel intimately acquainted, silence is, in fact, a domain about which we can hazard only guesses, guesses our scientists sometimes validate, while its former kingdom, the ineffable, continues to contract.

But even if silence remains forever beyond our reach, the notion of such a supposed emptiness is, like the placeholder zero, an object whose utility is inexhaustible—and whose value in a clamorous world soars.

II

2 SELLING SILENCE

"*. . . und wovon man nicht reden kann, darueber muss man schweigen.*" It seems a self-evident assertion (". . . and about that of which we cannot speak, we must remain silent"), Ludwig Wittgenstein's injunction in his 1922 *Tractatus Logico-Philosophicus* to respect the limits of language, beyond which lies, as the philosopher goes on to explain, nonsense. But silence is much more than the homage we offer ignorance, the abashed confession we sigh out of shame, the prayer we address to the ineffable.

Today silence is also a commodity, one bought and sold at prices rivaling our most sought-after consumer goods. "Let us have the luxury of silence," Jane Austen writes in *Mansfield Park*. Unfortunately, the cost of that luxury is increasingly beyond the means of most shoppers.

"So much of luxury now is about the sound of silence," acknowledges Jonah Disend of Redscout, the brand-development company, who points to cellphone-free retreats as an example. And Mark Ellwood describes the lengths to which Swiss luxury watchmaker Vacheron Constantin has gone to achieve silence in just one mechanism of a $409,900 wristwatch:

> Sound is central to Vacheron Constantin's newest masterpiece. Its technical team worked to create the purest chime possible, developing a silent speed regulator to minimize background noise. It uses tiny screws and rotors in its governor in place of the traditional lever-type system to eliminate even the faintest whir. So complex is this movement, called the flying strike governor, that only four Vacheron Constantin watchmakers are qualified to build it, each with at least 15 years' experience in horology.[1]

We may admire the elegance of Vacheron Constantin's solution in silencing such a tiny noise through ingenious horological engineering and the craftsmanship of master watchmakers, but most surcharges for silence profit those who have produced the noise we seek to escape.

Few industries have moved as aggressively to charge for the alleviation of the din they themselves generate as air transport. But while airlines have grown thuggish in extorting payment for formerly free amenities of travel, complaints about add-on fees seldom extend to the steep price of admission to their airport lounges, among the most successful of boutiques peddling silence.

To anyone who has weathered squawking public address announcements about gate changes or final boarding calls or picking up the nearest courtesy phone, to anyone who has cringed beneath a loudspeaker blaring Muzak or the narration of a CNN special on obesity in American pets, or to anyone who has been startled by a beeping cart bearing the disabled across a terminal, it will come as no surprise that the most welcoming feature of the airport lounge is the muted lighting and dampened sound that greet one in its reception vestibule. For beyond the free chips and fresh fruit, the complimentary soft drinks and house wines, and the selection of trade magazines offered for the guest's reading enjoyment, travelers primarily purchase respite from the bustle of the terminal.

The layout of such lounges segregates silent work areas from carpeted bars and soundproofed playrooms for children. Even in their most convivial areas, where television screens display market news and sporting matches, a hushed decorum is maintained, with outbursts a rarity. Offered by airlines to first-class ticket holders and frequent fliers who have purchased annual club memberships, airport lounges make clear both in their promotional literature and their discreet entrances that segregation of noise from silence is an expression of segregation by class.

American Airlines, for instance, explicitly markets its "Admirals Club" as an expression of rank: "Treat an Admirals Club lounge as an oasis of peace—away from all of the airport hustle. Because we know a little space to yourself can add up to a feeling, well, really big." The United Airlines Club promises that, for its $500 annual fee, you will be able to "Relax in a sophisticated environment when you wait for your flight." Not surprisingly, many clubs have dress codes.

The association of silence with wealth is not a recent marketing strategy, of course, but the marriage of tranquility and privilege is, in fact, the very purpose of airline lounges.

This reverence that silence pays affluence is even more obvious once the traveler ascends to the heavens, for noise can be subdued not merely in the airport but on the airplane itself. First introduced in 1986 for the protection of the hearing of pilots, Bose noise-canceling headphones have been used on NASA's space shuttle and on the International Space Station. Now available in consumer models starting at $300, these battery-powered headphones mute the roar of the massive jet engines just a few feet away. Having inherited a pair of these headphones from a deceased relative, I can attest personally to the extraordinary effect of this technology: one does arrive less exhausted from a cross-country flight when that journey occurs in near silence.

Of course, the Bose Corporation is well aware of how attractive silence will seem to fellow travelers during such a grueling flight. So each headphone case is equipped with a small sleeve stuffed with "Courtesy Cards" in French and in English to distribute to anyone asking how to get a pair.

Thus, for a $500 airline club membership and a $300 pair of noise-canceling headphones, one can travel the sky in silence, a luxury that—like most luxuries—begins to feel less a luxury and more a necessity the more often one indulges in its pleasures.

To be fair, I should admit that air travel sometimes offers a quiet voyage to those in every class of service. Of course, such interludes of stillness express something other than tranquility.

On a short hop from New Orleans to Houston early one morning, I and my fellow passengers were startled into worried silence as we raced down the runway by a nun who suddenly began to pray aloud the rosary, as if she knew something the rest of us did not. Others joined in her Hail Marys and Our Fathers as we were pressed against our seatbacks by the force of the takeoff. Only as the wheels tucked into the belly of the plane and we passed above ten thousand feet did a member of the crew explain over the intercom that many among us were on their way to Medjugorje, in what was then Yugoslavia, where the Virgin had appeared to six adolescents in 1981. These pilgrims, we learned, intended to pray all the way to Texas.

Though our anxious stillness gave way to relief on that short trip—at least once we knew the purpose of the prayers—an uninterrupted silence lasted until the plane touched down on a different flight a decade later.

Concluding a book tour, I was on a Friday afternoon flight home out of St. Louis. As we were ascending to our cruising altitude, the electrical system of the cabin flashed out in the middle of an announcement. We silently watched worried flight attendants hurry forward, but a moment later a crackle on the P.A. was followed by the pilot's calm voice explaining that we had blown one electrical system but would continue to New Orleans since the plane had triple redundancy on all essential systems. As he tried to put us at ease, he was interrupted as the second electrical system failed rather dramatically. When the third electrical system cut in and power was again restored, the pilot tersely informed us that we were heading back to St. Louis. That brief twenty-minute return occurred in what is quite troublingly called "dead silence." Not even the children aboard that plane made a sound until applause cheered the pilot as we touched down again in St. Louis.

So silence, in my experience, takes two forms in the air: luxury and terror. But flight is not the only mode of transport that demands a premium from its customers to mute the racket it creates.

In a 2014 comparison of fuel economy, for example, *Road & Track* magazine issued a surprising declaration: "America's most fuel-efficient new car isn't a Prius: You'll never believe what beats it." The magazine named a Mercedes the winner and went on to explain its choice. "We're not picking on the Prius (it's a technological marvel), but it's a car created solely for efficiency, and that shows in its road manners. The $52,634 E250 is a luxury car that just happens to get unbelievable mileage. It's 1001 pounds heavier than the Toyota but feels as if every ounce of that went toward noise cancellation and luxury."[2] Notice that "noise cancellation" is the one luxury singled out by the author.

Even more dramatic attention is paid to Mercedes noise cancellation in a 2015 article in *The Wall Street Journal*,

"Mercedes-Maybach S600: The Silence Is Deafening." In describing the incredibly quiet ride of this sedan with a base price of $190,275, the author explains the silence is not merely deafening; it is sickening:

> I'm getting woozy. Something about this car is playing havoc with my vestibular system. . . .
>
> The rear cabin, the company claims, is the quietest ever in a production car. In fact, Daimler developed the aero acoustics in its new wind tunnel with rolling road, which is able to conduct experiments with angled flows of air and crosswinds. The larger the door—and the Maybach has some big ones—the more likely a crosswind may pull the door away from the frame, creating small acoustical hot spots. That's why the door seals look like rolled-up wetsuits.
>
> In any event, wind noise is virtually nonexistent. Tire noise and vibration barely palpable. And then I realize the feeling. It's simulator sickness.
>
> This condition is common to even experienced pilots training in simulators with wraparound 3-D screens that tell their brains one thing while their inner ear tells them something else. The Mercedes-Maybach S600 is so attenuated, so muffled and muted, it turns down the sense data to the point where things almost don't compute, at least from the back seat.[3]

The rich, apparently, are willing to endure even nausea for the luxury of silence.

But if silence sickens the rich, noise is an affliction of the poor. Alex Lockwood, in a *Counterfire* review of John Stewart's *Why Noise Matters* (published by Earthscan in 2011), points out the disproportionate effect of noise on those living in poverty:

> At around 50 decibels people begin to get annoyed with daytime noise (at night, it is 30 decibels). At around 55 decibels (a 10 decibel increase represents a doubling of sound levels) people become extremely annoyed. Above 130dbs is the human threshold of pain, although the gradual loss of hearing from continuous noise is a greater worldwide problem. One of the strengths of *Why Noise Matters* is that it offers up noise pollution as a global phenomenon. While its research is not (and does not claim to be) comprehensive, this global approach highlights the inequities in experiences of noise pollution between rich and poor, industrialised and industrialising, and asks why more is not being done to tackle noise as a social injustice. Noise is, as are other forms of pollution, a class issue.

For example, a MORI survey (2003) revealed that almost 20% of people in the UK, with a household income of less than £17,500, regularly hear noise from neighbours, including 93% of social housing tenants. In contrast only 12% of people with an income of more than £30,000 could hear their neighbours. Looked at globally, the divide between the peaceful rich and harried poor gets bigger according to where people live. In nearly all countries, from industrialised nations such as the UK, through to India, Thailand and across Africa, because poor people are more likely to live closer to major sources of noise pollution (roads, airports, industry), they suffer disproportionately more annoyance. Noise is not only the forgotten pollutant, but is increasingly what Les Blomberg, executive director of the Noise Pollution Clearing House, calls "second hand noise." More and more, it is not created by those who suffer from it.[4]

The hushed halls of affluence buffer the rich from the hubbub of poverty, but for the poor, the clatter of modern life—like other forms of pollution—is inescapable. And as noise continues its inexorable advance into the quietest eddies of wilderness, even the rich may find a silent retreat impossible to locate.

3 SEEKING SILENCE

Larry Blake, owner of Swelltone Labs in New Orleans, has supervised the post-production sound for over fifty films including *Contagion*, *The Informant!*, *Syriana*, *Ocean's Eleven*, *Out of Sight*, and *Traffic*. In trying to find background silence for *The Knick*, a television series set in New York in the early 1900s, Blake first tried the shooting location itself in the streets of Brooklyn, with all traffic silent for a few blocks, but that was not still enough. Among the other venues he went to in search of neutral air, void of modern life and insects, were the winter swamplands of southern Louisiana. But even there, it was difficult to locate a spot not tainted with the buzz of machinery—an air conditioner, a car engine, a boat motor, a tractor, a lawn mower. With all the sound-editing tricks technology offers, recording the kind of silences that surrounded human beings a hundred years ago requires great ingenuity.[1]

Even then, it was not so easy. In his *Meditations on Quixote*, published a century ago in 1914, José Ortega y Gasset recounts the difficulty, the impossibility, of finding silence:

There are places which enjoy a wonderful silence—which is never absolute silence. When all around is completely quiet, the noiseless void which remains must be occupied by something, and then we hear the pounding of our own hearts, the throbbing of the blood in our temples, the flow of air which floods into our lungs and then rushes out. All this is disturbing because it has too concrete a meaning. Each heartbeat sounds as if it were to be our last. The following beat which saves us always seems to come accidentally and does not guarantee the next one. That is why it is preferable to have a silence in which purely decorative, unidentifiable sounds are heard.[2]

Contemporary science confirms Ortega's frustration in his attempt to arrive at "absolute silence":

The quietest place on earth, an anechoic chamber at Orfield Laboratories in Minnesota, is so quiet that the longest anybody has been able to bear it is 45 minutes.

Inside the room it's silent. So silent that the background noise measured is actually negative decibels, -9.4 dBA. Steven Orfield, the lab's founder, told *Hearing Aid Know*: "We challenge people to sit in the chamber in the dark—one person stayed in there for 45 minutes. When it's quiet, ears will adapt. The quieter the room, the more things you hear. You'll hear your heart beating, sometimes you can hear your lungs, hear your stomach gurgling loudly. In the anechoic chamber, you become the sound."[3]

One of the insights that have emerged in the lab's anechoic chamber is that silence "is a very disorientating experience. Mr. Orfield explained that it's so disconcerting that sitting down is a must. He said: 'How you orient yourself is through sounds you hear when you walk. In the anechoic chamber, you don't have any cues. You take away the perceptual cues that allow you to balance and manoeuvre. If you're in there for half an hour, you have to be in a chair.'"[4]

This spatial disorientation would not come as a surprise to those suddenly struck deaf. George Prochnik relates a conversation with Dirksen Bauman, a professor of deaf cultural studies at Gallaudet University, about people who had experienced sudden hearing loss. "I assumed he was going to describe the psychological experience of being suddenly cast into silence. In fact, each person in this group, recounting their initial shock at having gone deaf, commented that they did not think to themselves, 'Oh how terrible—I can't hear anything.' Rather, what they experienced was a deep sense of '*Where am I?*'"[5]

Earlier in his book, Prochnik quotes Supreme Court justice Felix Frankfurter: "The men whose labors brought forth the Constitution of the United States had the street outside Independence Hall covered with earth so that their deliberations might not be disturbed by passing traffic. Our democracy presupposed the deliberative process as a condition of thought and of responsible choice by the electorate."[6] Unable to find a quiet place to work even two centuries ago, the framers of the Constitution constructed one.

The effort to establish a zone of silence continues to engage us. One Square Inch is an organization dedicated to preserving the silence of, as its name suggests, one square inch of forest. That small bit of woods the size of a postage stamp is intended to be, in Ortega's words, one of those "places which enjoy a wonderful silence."

One Square Inch of Silence is the quietest place in the United States. Located in the Hoh Rain Forest at Olympic National Park, it is 3.2 miles from the Visitor's Center above Mt. Tom Creek Meadows on the Hoh River Trail. Hiking time from the parking lot at the Visitor's Center to the site is approximately two hours along a gentle path lined by ancient trees and ferns. The exact location is marked by a small red-colored stone placed on top of a moss-covered log at 47° 51.959N, 123° 52.221W, 678 feet above sea level. Directions to the site can be found on the links page.

One Square Inch of Silence was designated on Earth Day 2005 (April 22, 2005) to protect and manage the natural soundscape in Olympic Park's backcountry wilderness. The logic is simple; if a loud noise, such as the passing of an aircraft, can impact many square miles, then a natural place, if maintained in a 100% noise-free condition, will also impact many square miles around it. It is predicted that protecting a single square inch of land from noise pollution will benefit large areas of the park.[7]

So we have been reduced to saving one square inch of silence for us as well as for future generations. But, of course, we're really not talking about silence. One Square Inch simply wants to eliminate human noise so we can hear the sounds of nature. And perhaps that's just as well, since an encounter with actual silence would leave us unable to stand, as Orfield's anechoic chamber demonstrates.

In the end, the search for silence may be an attempt to escape what we are. Ortega was not the only writer to recognize this conundrum. In his brief play entitled *Silence*, Harold Pinter poses the fundamental contradiction humans face in seeking silence: "Around me sits the night. Such a silence. I can hear myself. Cup my ear. My heart beats in my ear. Such a silence. Is it me? Am I silent or speaking? How can I know? Can I know such things?"[8]

4 SILENCE VERSUS SOLITUDE

We assume that solitude is the setting of silence, but one is often merely the concomitant of the other. A brief survey of the two suggests that silence is usually a late articulation of solitude, one whose value begins to trump solitude's importance only as the pressures that engendered such isolation yield to more extreme circumstances or intentions.

Enforced solitude through shipwreck or abandonment by one's fellows, such as the adventures of Robinson Crusoe or the exile of Philoctetes on the island of Lemnos by Greek warriors headed for Troy, is an ancient literary staple that remains popular. Today, though, in a world intent on turning all its desert islands into Club Meds for the masses or private luxury retreats for celebrities, an author needs a great deal of ingenuity to engineer the requisite circumstances that result in an individual waking to solitude on some uninhabited foreign shore.

Beset by rapid urban growth and other attendant ills of the Industrial Revolution, the nineteenth and early twentieth centuries seem to have fostered a compulsion, at least in the West, to find solitude. No doubt influenced by the sentimentalization of nature in the embrace of primitivism in the preceding centuries, both European and American writers railed against the ills of crowded city life and urged a return to the supposed solitude of the countryside.

We may take this theme to be a contribution of the Romantics, but they are acutely aware of having been divorced from nature. As William Wordsworth laments in his sonnet "The World Is Too Much with Us," "Little we see in Nature that is ours," and so he yearns for a lost paradise: "Great God! I'd rather be/A Pagan suckled in a creed outworn." He does not suggest, though, that he could find his way back to such derelict belief, especially in a country where carefully tended gardens merely pretended at the unkempt vitality of the wild.

In the still expanding United States, however, much wilderness lay beyond the plowed fields of the settled East. And even there beginning on the Fourth of July 1845, Henry David Thoreau could live a simple and somewhat solitary life in the woods surrounding Walden Pond in Massachusetts.

Mark Twain's Huck Finn shares Thoreau's aversion to civilization and preference for the natural world: "But I reckon I got to light out for the Territory ahead of the rest, because Aunt Sally she's going to adopt me and sivilize me, and I can't stand it. I been there before."

Writing just four years after the 1884 publication of *The Adventures of Huckleberry Finn*, yet another great writer,

William Butler Yeats, succinctly expresses the desire to escape the modern world and its "pavements grey" in "The Lake Isle of Innisfree":

> I will arise and go now, and go to Innisfree,
> And a small cabin build there, of clay and wattles made:
> Nine bean-rows will I have there, a hive for the honey-bee;
> And live alone in the bee-loud glade.
>
> And I shall have some peace there, for peace comes dropping slow,
> Dropping from the veils of the morning to where the cricket sings;
> There midnight's all a glimmer, and noon a purple glow,
> And evening full of the linnet's wings.
>
> I will arise and go now, for always night and day
> I hear lake water lapping with low sounds by the shore;
> While I stand on the roadway, or on the pavements grey,
> I hear it in the deep heart's core.

In retreating to nature, the nineteenth century hoped to find at least stillness, if not silence.

But contradictorily the dread of abandonment and enforced solitude was just as keenly felt as the desire to escape the noisy throngs of the city. Edgar Allan Poe's "The Cask of Amontillado," published in 1846, recounts a ghastly act of vengeance in which the aggrieved narrator immures his foolish rival, costumed in a jester's motley and belled cap for Carnival, in moldering Venetian catacombs. Demanding some acknowledgment from his victim before he forces the final stone into place, the cunning villain is chilled by the answer he receives: "There came forth in return only a jingling of the bells." An earlier, lesser known of Poe's stories, "The Premature Burial," speaks even more directly of the nineteenth-century fear of being buried alive. The story's terrified narrator resorts to a version of Bateson's Belfry, a bell connected by a rope to the hand of the interred that might summon help if the presumed dead should awaken in the coffin. So widespread were such fears among Victorians that a Society for the Prevention of People Being Buried Alive was established.[1]

Contemporaneous with this strange phenomenon was the introduction of solitary confinement, first implemented, at least in the United States, in 1829 at the Eastern State Penitentiary in Philadelphia. A similar regimen, but including complete silence, was introduced about the same time at the Auburn Prison in New York.

As Michel Foucault notes in *Discipline & Punish: The Birth of the Prison*, the Philadelphia model depended upon the isolation of the prisoner for reformation, and the Auburn model allowed communal activity with other prisoners but only in absolute silence. Foucault goes on to remark that "solitude is the primary condition of total submission." But he recognizes that silence is the fundamental weapon wielded against the recalcitrance of the inmate, whether through solitary isolation and "the silent architecture that confronted" the prisoner or the complete silence of the Auburn system, "which was guaranteed by surveillance and punishment."[2]

The disastrous results of these practices prompted US Supreme Court Justice Samuel Freeman Miller to find in Medley, 134 U.S. 160, the following: "A considerable number of the prisoners fell, after even a short confinement, into a semi-fatuous condition, from which it was next to impossible to arouse them, and others became violently insane; others still, committed suicide; while those who stood the ordeal better were not generally reformed, and in most cases did not recover sufficient mental activity to be of any subsequent service to the community."[3] (Hans Christian Andersen visited in 1851 a Swedish prison modeled on the Philadelphia experiment; he noted that "a silence deep as the grave rests over it. . . . It is all a well-built machine, a nightmare for the spirit.")[4]

Despite such criticism, as of 2005, forty states in the United States were found to operate more than sixty "supermax" prisons with isolation units that lock prisoners in their cells in solitary confinement 23 hours a day with no communal yard time.[5] California, alone, incarcerates 12,000 inmates in long-term isolation.[6] Following a Justice Department report that New York City's Rikers Island kept up to 25 percent of adolescent prisoners in solitary confinement—some for more than six months—the City of New York in 2015 banned solitary confinement for prisoners twenty-one years old and younger. About the same time, members of the American Institute of Architects petitioned the organization to censure architects who design cells for solitary confinement or death chambers; the petition was rejected.[7] Despite growing awareness of the actual effects on inmates, prison authorities continue to rely on solitude and silence as the most extreme forms of punishment, short of execution, to reform behavior.

Such exclusion from society—whether penal imprisonment, political exile, or religious ostracism—is an ancient remedy for the community's unwanted. But a new version of exclusion as a luxury of the wealthy was introduced by Anton Chekhov in "The Bet."

This 1889 short story opens one dark autumn night as an old banker recalls a party he hosted fifteen years earlier in which a debate on whether capital punishment or life imprisonment was more humane results in a bet. Annoyed by the intransigence of a lawyer who argues on behalf of imprisonment, the rich banker wages two million rubles that the young man cannot spend fifteen years in solitary confinement, deprived of receiving letters or newspapers and neither speaking nor hearing human voices. The confined is allowed a piano, books, wine, and tobacco, but he must communicate all his needs in writing through a little window constructed for this purpose in the cell established for him in a wing of the banker's house, where he can be constantly observed. The fifteen years pass without a violation of the rules, and the old banker, having lost his fortune, intends to murder the voluntary prisoner before the bet can be collected the next day. But in the sleeping prisoner's cell, the banker finds a letter declaring the years of reading have revealed everything about human life to the lawyer and left him full of contempt for the values of the world. He concludes by renouncing his winnings. The next day he flees his prison before the terms of the bet are fulfilled, and the banker locks the letter of renunciation in a safe.[8]

There are reasons why a piece of literature is written in one century rather than another, and there are reasons why a particular plot finds similar expression by more than one author in a given moment. Perhaps Chekhov intended the story as a moral reprimand to readers or as a portrait of a secular saint who comes to transcend materialism through a voluntary retreat from the world—even if, as the old banker thinks, it was the lawyer's avarice that ushered him into his cell at the beginning. But something incidental in "The Bet" found its way into an unexpected place: *The Twilight Zone*.

An episode of the American television series, "The Silence" dramatizes a similar bet, though as its title suggests, the wager is not about remaining imprisoned but remaining silent. Colonel Archie Taylor, exasperated by the incessant chatter of a fellow member of his men's club, Jamie Tennyson, bets $500,000 that the young man cannot go without speaking for a year. Monitored in a glass cell within the club, Tennyson manages to remain silent, even when the colonel, in an effort to call off the bet, tempts him with money and torments him with rumors of his wife's infidelity. Having successfully passed the year, Tennyson silently extends his hand for payment, but Colonel Taylor is forced to admit his fortune was lost years ago, and so he cannot pay the $500,000. In consternation, Tennyson scribbles a final note for the colonel to read aloud to the members of the club: "I knew I would not be able to keep my part of the bargain, so one year ago I had the nerves to my vocal cords severed." He then lowers his ascot to reveal the scar across his throat.

Though some commentators suggest the 1961 episode was based upon the Chekhov story, the script's author, Rod Serling, maintained in a lecture at Ithaca College that he was unfamiliar with "The Bet" when he wrote "The Silence." He did note that such a plot could send a character in many possible directions.[9] That Chekhov should focus on solitude (with silence merely an attendant condition) and Serling, on silence itself reflects a transformation of societal concerns over the seventy-two years that separate "The Bet" from "The Silence."

Intervening in 1922 was Franz Kafka's "A Hunger Artist." Sharing voluntary incarceration and public monitoring of self-denial with both the Chekhov and the Serling stories, Kafka's tale of an artist whose extended fasts draw attention as the performances of a kind of sideshow freak has been recognized as a twentieth-century masterpiece and finds contemporary resonance in Tehching Hsieh's "Cage Piece."

On September 30, 1978, Mr. Hsieh entered a sparsely furnished wooden cell he had constructed in his loft, had it secured with paper seals by his lawyer to confirm that he never left the space, and spent the next year confined there without a television or a radio, never talking, writing, or reading.[10] He had himself photographed each day and allowed the public to observe him once or twice a month from 11:00 a.m. to 5:00 p.m. Returning on September 29, 1979, his lawyer affirmed that all seals were intact, and the artist exited his cage, having spent an entire year "doing absolutely nothing," according to *New York Times* art critic Roberta Smith in a review of this and the four other "One Year Performances" Mr. Hsieh would go on to offer. Ms. Smith likens his project to that of "a fanatical devotee of some religion" but concludes that the artist's subject is "the almost palpable immensity and emptiness of time, nothing but time, of life as the filling of time. . . . Mr. Hsieh did not make his life his art. Instead, with Classical precision and unquestionable monstrousness, he expanded his art until it fully occupied, consumed and suspended his life."[11]

In "Kafka and the Hunger Artists," Breon Mitchell documents the existence of historical hunger artists, such as Giovanni Succi, a professional Italian faster who was the subject of articles and photographs published in 1896 by *Das interessante Blatt*.[12] The practice seems to have died out around the beginning of the First World War, though references exist to contemporary hunger artists as late as 1956. Is it a coincidence that, in a period of sufficiency, when the ancient specter of famine has yielded to confidence in the food supply, a nostalgia for hunger should express itself in exhibitions of fasting? Only a century earlier, as Georges Lefebvre has argued in *The Great Fear of 1789*, panic precipitated by drought and rumors of impending food shortages fueled the revolutionary uprising in France that summer.

So, is it not possible that the focus on silence rather than solitude in the twentieth century—whether in Rod Serling's "The Silence" or Tehching Hsieh's "Cage Piece"—may be a form of nostalgia as well? Both confined men are under frequent observation, so they are not deprived of association with other human beings. They simply may not speak. In a world of fewer and fewer sanctuaries of silence, are we not nostalgic for a quieter world where blaring radios, nattering televisions, crackling loudspeakers, screeching car alarms, ringing telephones, whining motors, grumbling air conditioners, humming refrigerators, roaring airplanes overhead, and all the other sonic intrusions introduced into our lives by the Machine Age did not drown out the "bee-loud" solitude Yeats already misses in 1888?

What a contradiction is this solitary silence we so deeply value even as we argue it should be banned as an intolerably cruel punishment! Is the essential difference between that silence we seek and that which we fear simply the difference between the voluntary and the involuntary?

5 VOLUNTARY SILENCES

Voluntary isolation to pursue spiritual refinement is a traditional element of many religions. Like Gautama Buddha and Lao-Tzu, many religious figures have spent at least part of their lives as hermits, a word derived from the Greek for "of the desert" and, by extension, "solitude." The Medieval anchorite tradition differs from earlier forms of eremitic practice in its commitment to spend the rest of one's life in a cell attached to a church, sometimes with only a small window called a "squint" to receive the Eucharist during Mass; so absolute was this commitment of the anchorite or anchoress that he or she would be consecrated with funeral rites, signifying that the individual was henceforth dead to the world.

None of these practices mandated silence. In fact, many such cells, or anchorholds, had a second window facing away from the church where the anchorite could dispense wisdom to the faithful. So though one might expect solitude to breed silence, only infrequently has asceticism demanded it. In early monastic communities "but also among solitaries, silence was only one strategy among several in the pursuit and performance of contemplation."[1]

Biblical accounts vary little about Jesus's forty days in the wilderness. Matthew, Mark, and Luke agree that, in preparation for his ministry, Jesus spends forty days fasting in the desert. Mark writes that he lives in solitude among the wild beasts and angels minister to him. The synoptic evangelists also agree that he is tested three times by Satan. Failing to tempt Jesus, the devil leaves him, in Luke's words, "until an opportune time." Those forty days of silence are interrupted only by Satan's temptations, but the gospels draw no attention to that silence. In fact, as late as the third century, Christianity was still debating the role of silence. Clement of Alexandria, Tertullian, and Cyprian, the bishop of Carthage, all attempted to legitimize silent prayer, but the Emperor Justinian, three centuries later, "forbade liturgical prayers in the administration of the sacraments to be uttered silently."[2]

So the association of silence and spirituality in ancient religious practice is not as certain as we might expect. By the sixteenth century, though, St. John of the Cross speaks for many when he asserts that "Silence is God's first language." Four hundred years later, that notion is widespread when Mother Teresa writes, "In the silence of the heart God speaks."

One of the earliest sustained efforts to integrate silence into religious devotion was led by Odo, the second abbot of Cluny, where over the next few centuries monastic sign language was developed to replace the necessity of everyday speech.[3] Even today, Benedictines continue to honor the legacy of Cluny where possible, as I learned firsthand.

I was a fourteen-year-old studying for the priesthood in a Benedictine monastery when, in a mere three days, religious conviction curdled into doubt.

You might assume that my misgivings were engendered by the hypocrisy of the monks who taught us or by implausible dogmas. But those monks seemed to me at the time serious men sincerely dedicated to a difficult vocation—and I've learned nothing since to alter my view of them. As for belief in miracles, it's not so difficult a leap of the imagination for an adolescent only a few years out of childhood, especially when the adults he admires profess those same beliefs.

So it was neither the inconstancy of my teachers in their vows nor the doctrines to which I was asked to subscribe that unraveled my faith. In fact, it was nothing I saw or heard. Rather, it was something I didn't hear.

Seven other boys from my New Orleans Catholic elementary school entered the seminary with me. We traveled the 24-mile causeway across Lake Pontchartrain to a Benedictine monastery surrounded by a thousand acres of pine forest. The first night, sharing an open dormitory, we fell asleep in the dark to the intermittent sobbing of fellow high-school freshmen, homesick for their mothers.

It was a rigorous life for a teenager. Up each morning at 5:30 for a half hour of silent meditation, we ate a breakfast of warm bread baked by monks and of eggs raised on the monastery's farm. Classes started at 7:30 six days a week, with a curriculum not so different from other high schools—except, of course, for theology and Latin and Gregorian chant. We attended mass at midday, sang vespers in the evening. We watched no television that first year nor listened to a radio. Our parents were allowed to visit one Sunday a month.

Even as I describe it, I'm struck by how harsh a life it sounds for a fourteen-year-old to follow. Yet I can only describe the experience of that year as joyful. The simple rule of the Benedictine order, "*ora et labora*" ("pray and work"), elevated every action to a form of praise. Nothing we did was meaningless, whether scouring our dormitories for weekly inspections or cleaning stalls in a barn or threading rosaries at night for missionaries in Guatemala.

In the spring, as Easter approached, we were instructed that we would undertake a silent retreat. For three days we would not speak. Those of us raised in cities had been shocked by the profound darkness of the forest on a moonless night. In silence, we were about to discover another kind of darkness with which we were unacquainted.

The modern world hums. What we take for silence is simply the buzz we tolerate as "white noise." Imagine, though, if from the static always trembling in our ears we could tweeze out the lawn mower whining across the summer lawn, the automobile purring in the driveway, the chattering television set chuckling in the next room, the refrigerator grumbling on and shuddering off, the air conditioner growling like an old dog in its sleep, and finally, one by one, every human voice. You would welcome it, wouldn't you—that utter stillness?

But as an adolescent, I found silence offered no more illumination than did darkness.

What was it like? Enforced silence, I discovered seven years later when I joined a hunger strike in college, is a great deal like starvation. The first day, encouraged by others who have pledged not to eat again until concessions are won, the faster feels elation. But euphoria over that common cause yields to preoccupation with the body when one wakes the second day to the insistent desire for food. Still, even if others are sneaking off to wolf down a candy bar, a dedicated individual can resist the temptation. By the third day—just the third day!—the point of the strike has been obscured by the swelling distraction of hunger, hunger more demanding of satisfaction than any pang of desire ever before felt.

The Canadian poet George Jonas opens *The Happy Hungry Man*, a volume of his poems, with lines he attributes to Dibil el Khuzai: "And is the hungry man not happy? for is he not unfettered of the passions that enslave us? or is his desire not capable of fulfilment? and are the many mysteries of Allah not reduced for him but to a single one?"[4]

For me, Allah, Yahweh, God became the single mystery to which my silence reduced the world. Adrift on a flat sea that stretched in every direction to an unbroken horizon,

I floated, waiting for another voice to break the still surface. But no voice reached me. I felt, for the first time in my life, forsaken.

If silence is a kind of hunger, what can possibly satisfy its gnawing? Not mere noise—that, in its own way, is another kind of silence. On the edge of the forest as evening began to cast shadows over a monastery that had been, except for prayers, voiceless for three days, I realized the emptiness of the air craved nothing but words.

Remember: I was only a teenager, as ill prepared to endure silence as to live long with hunger. The adolescent appetite is legendary, after all, but not just for food. I devoured books, for example, though I found myself circumscribed in my reading by the *Index Librorum Prohibitorum*—the Index of Forbidden Books—silencing centuries of voices and still maintained then by the church. But even a censored library, like the garden, has a serpent or two coiled beneath its apple trees hissing rebellion.

A year later, my father received a letter from a seminary prefect cautioning him that I had grown cynical and pessimistic with a dangerous tendency to counterpose truth and obedience. I lasted another six months before I transferred to a high school in the city, where I eventually won a writing contest and a college scholarship as an English major. I had begun high school seeking answers; I graduated with a new vocation, dedicated to posing questions.

We might dispute whether a seven-year-old has achieved, as Catholic doctrine maintains, the age of reason. But who would disagree that a teenager has entered the age of loss? Virginity is not the only innocence sacrificed on the altar of experience in that second decade of life. An adolescent's certainty, too, can darken into doubt—particularly in the hollow heart of silence.

III

6 THE REPRESENTATION OF SILENCE

Conventions enforce silence—or at least what we take for silence—without ambiguity about their intended purpose. Hands clapped over the mouth, or even a finger pressed to the lips, will leave no doubt that one has entered a zone of silence. Similarly, the palms extended toward an audience to hush its applause, the clinking of fork against goblet to silence the din of a dinner party, and the shushing that gently requests quiet of a stranger are rarely misunderstood. Though most such conventions assume a human voice as the source of unwelcomed sound, a red circle with a diagonal slash across its diameter superimposed upon the drawing of a bullhorn or a loudspeaker extends the prohibition against noise to mechanical amplifiers.

We know how to signal silence. We even know how to spell it: shh. The representation of silence itself, though, challenges writers, composers, and artists.

Is the black page that follows the death of Yorick in Laurence Sterne's *The Life and Opinions of Tristram Shandy, Gentleman* an illustration of grief, or is it mere funereal bunting? Or is it, perhaps, a moment of silence imposed by the author on the loquacious narrator of his novel to honor the passing of a character? Of course, it is easy enough to imagine the concluding page of the novel's twelfth chapter and its verso as a representation of the dark silence of death, as eyes and ears close on the world. If so, is darkness a cognate of silence?

But then, the blank white page that follows the narrator's invitation to the reader to sketch his or her own conception of the Widow Wadman at the opening of the thirty-eighth chapter of the sixth volume is an interruption of Sterne's cascading words and, therefore, also a pause, a silence. The author leaves no doubt that blank silence is superior to any utterance he himself might make in its place: "Thrice happy book! Thou wilt have one page, at least, within thy covers, which MALICE will not blacken, and which IGNORANCE cannot misrepresent."

Is a white page, rather than a dark leaf, the better representation of silence? Or will we allow both unsullied whiteness and unrelieved darkness to serve as contradictory images of silence? And what of *Tristram Shandy's* marbled sheet that interrupts the narration between the early insertion of the black page and the late appearance of the white?

Perhaps the distinction, then, is not one of color but of background versus foreground. In reading, after all, we vocalize the black marks that rake the white paper upon which they are impressed, silencing our voices—if only briefly—to communicate the spaces between words. The white paper is silence against which the black ink is understood to be sound. But we would read white words against a black sheet in exactly the same way. So does reading assume that language is embroidered upon silence, that silence is the backdrop of speech?

Though speech depends upon that assumption, reading does not. *Scriptio continua*, which employs neither spaces nor other signifiers between words, was common in the classical world and remains in use in various Asian languages. Similarly, Internet conventions such as email addresses and the URLs of websites treat unmarked spaces between words as unreadable. Apparently, legibility does not necessarily require the representation of the silence from which the word is distinguished. But the translation of the legible into speech does demand subtle integrations of silence.

Sterne is as much a typographer as a writer in his masterwork, extensively employing dashes, asterisks, and other typographical devices (including even an occasional printer's fist); the reader will render most of these punctuation marks by silence. As any grammarian could explain, three evenly spaced ellipsis points, for example, indicate an omission, a lacuna, in a quoted text and therefore ought to be acknowledged in reading aloud by the introduction of a silence of some sort. We do not trouble ourselves over what sort of silence should be used to distinguish ellipsis points from the period, the semicolon, the colon, the parenthesis, the dash, and the comma. Silence, after all, is not the purpose of punctuation; structure is. But to hear a trained actor read aloud is to learn how distinctive—and therefore eloquent—each silence may be.

The most eloquent use of punctuation establishes, in poetry, a silence that pauses the momentum of the poem's meter. Called a caesura, it is represented in scansion by a pair of vertical parallel lines. One of the most heartbreaking examples comes in the final line of the third quatrain of John Keats's "When I Have Fears," a lament the consumptive young poet offers in the face of his impending death. Having expressed his regret in the first two quatrains of the sonnet over the literature he will not live to pen, he then turns to the loss of the woman he loves. Keats is so overcome with emotion that he cannot complete the final line of the quatrain, stopping himself with a caesura:

And when I feel, fair creature of an hour,
That I shall never look upon thee more,
Never have relish in the faery power
Of unreflecting love!—then on the shore
Of the wide world I stand alone, and think
Till love and fame to nothingness do sink.

As the poet falters in contemplating their separation, his voice is extinguished, if only for a moment, by a silence that prematurely ends the first part of the sonnet in mid-line (and surely foreshadows the final, abrupt silencing of his voice that he rightly fears). Though he finds consolation of a sort in the poem's resolution, the caesura, that sudden silence embedded in the center of the sonnet's twelfth line, may well be the most expressive moment of "When I Have Fears."

Just as silence and sound are intertwined in language, so also are they paired in music; and composers have invented a system of musical notation that, at least in its representation of silence, does not differ significantly from written language. Where a novelist might use a period, the composer inserts a rest. Rendered in the same ink as the notes that precede and follow it, the squiggle of the quarter rest distinguishes itself from the silence of the white page in a manner similar to the marks of punctuation just discussed.

Like punctuation, though, rests are not so simple as they might appear. Voice students are taught to sing through a rest, even if that singing is not vocalized. Jazz musicians, too, play through the silences, even if we can't hear those inaudible notes. The rest is an element of the composition, not a break from it. In fact, a rest has a fixed duration—a duration equivalent to a whole, half, quarter, or eighth note; it is a defined silence integral to the structure of the work. Appearing among a sequence of notes, the rest—sharing duration, if not pitch, timbre, and intensity with those other notes—could be understood to signify the note that is never played. So a composer deploys silence very much as a writer punctuates a sentence, which is to say as a means of asserting structural relationships among the constituent elements of a piece.

At a performance I attended last night of Franz Liszt's *Les Préludes*, the conductor prefaced the concert by wondering aloud if pizzicato is the musical equivalent of a question mark. Of course, Liszt's symphonic poem attempts to translate the poetry of Alphonse de Lamartine for an orchestra, so the listener is well justified in seeking correspondences between written verse (including even its punctuation) and musical technique. If pizzicato can be heard as a question mark, is the musical rest any less eloquent than the semicolon or the dash? For like punctuation marks, the rest doesn't express silence; silence is merely the expression of what the typographical device articulates.

Numerous examples can be offered. Liszt's punctuation with rests of his *Sonata in B minor* is an obvious instance, even to a casual listener. Similarly, the rest that follows each of the first two chords in Beethoven's *Third Symphony* certainly has the effect of an exclamation point on the audience.

Of course, a rest is not the only means by which a musician can signify the introduction of a silence into a composition. As in poetry, composers also have at their disposal the caesura, noted by paired slashes (often referred to as "railway tracks") and sometimes associated with the "grand pause." The grand pause, indicated by a fermata above a rest, extends the silence at the performer's discretion. Although rarely noted in the opening of a composition, a grand pause is often added by a soloist at the beginning of a performance. In

Bruno Monsaingeon's 1998 documentary, *Richter L'Insoumis*, the great Russian pianist Sviatoslav Richter recalls the most important lesson by his teacher at the Moscow Conservatory, Heinrich Neuhaus: "In the Liszt sonata, he taught me one essential thing: the silences. How to make silences sound. I have devised a little trick. You come on stage and sit down. Without a motion, and in silence, you count up to thirty. And then there's a kind of panic in the audience. 'What's going on?' And only after that long silence, that first *G*."

One composer has even employed the grand pause on his tombstone. The grave of the Russian composer Alfred Schnittke in Novodevichye Cemetery in Moscow is surmounted by a stone on which is engraved a rest beneath a fermata with a triple forte noted at the bottom: A very, very loud extended silence.

The various scores of John Cage's *4'33"* are useful examples of possible representations of silence. As the reader may know, *4'33"* is a composition that consists entirely of rests. David Tudor, publicly playing the piece for the first time on August 29, 1952, began his performance by closing the keyboard cover over the keys. Guided by a stopwatch, the pianist signaled the break between the three movements of the composition by silently opening and then closing again the keyboard cover. Although the original blank score has been lost, in 1989 Tudor reconstructed the sheet music he had quietly turned with one hand as he cupped a stopwatch in his other that summer evening nearly forty years earlier at the Maverick Concert Hall near Woodstock, New York. The penciled beats per minute and 4/4 time signature above blank staves and three decimal notations along the right margin (plus a page number in the lower right corner) are the only marks the composer has made to guide the performer.[1]

A note by John Cage to Henmar Press's 1960 edition indicates the duration of each movement; the score itself has become simply three Roman numerals, each followed by "TACET." Earlier, Cage's 1953 Kremen manuscript, now held by the Museum of Modern Art, rendered the silences of the three movements as vertical lines dividing white pages into sections, with the duration of the movements noted along the axis of the lines.[2] Perhaps inspired by Cage's note to the Henmar Press edition that "the work may be performed by an instrumentalist or combination of instrumentalists and last any length of time," a tongue-in-cheek 2012 arrangement for brass quintet by Frank Leonard uses three trebles and two bass clefs, each of their staffs limited to a centered whole rest surmounted by a fermata.[3]

As Leonard demonstrates, conventional scoring of the piece is possible. Cage himself, though, abandoned such traditional notation in favor of alternative visual renderings with verbal instructions to musicians about how to perform a bit more than four and a half minutes of silence. Cage's interest in exploring new systems for scoring music resulted in *Notations*, a 1969 collection of modern music manuscripts he edited. As the volume demonstrates, he was not the only composer to experiment with innovative representations of sound and silence. Nestled nearly halfway through the book is a sheet of blank song paper with a scrawled message at the bottom to "return to C E Ives Redding Conn." The blank page, nearly identical to Tudor's reconstructed sheet music from the premiere of Cage's composition, suggests that Charles Ives, perhaps unintentionally, had written a silent composition decades before *4'33"* and had employed the same form as Cage used initially to represent the absence of music: empty staves.

A similar score of twenty-four blank measures was presented by Alphonse Allais, a friend of Erik Satie, as his 1897 *Funeral March for the Obsequies of a Great Deaf Man*. (It should be noted that Allais was a French humorist, not a composer.) In listing antecedents, we must include Erwin Schulhoff's 1919 *Fünf Pittoresken* for piano; its silent *In futurum* section is composed entirely of rests.[4] And Kyle Gann has unearthed a 1932 cartoon from *The Etude* magazine for pianists in which a recalcitrant boy "gets out of practicing by composing a piece entirely of rests. What makes the coincidence uncanny is the name of the cartoonist: Hy Cage."[5] (These predecessors do not diminish John Cage's accomplishment. After all, as Henry David Thoreau reminded listeners at the Concord Lyceum in 1843, even Homer had his Homer and Orpheus, his Orpheus.)[6]

Of course, Cage argues that *4'33"* is not a performance of silence but a framing of incidental noises, "simply an act of listening."[7] However, just as we turn a blind eye both to the wall and to the frame around a painting, accepting their temporary invisibility as we focus on the canvas, so also do we turn a deaf ear if at all possible to the old man behind us in the auditorium wheezing through the piano sonata performed on stage. Cage may wish to incorporate into *4'33"* every creak, cough, and crinkle in the music hall, but they pass for silence in most concerts. He has not framed those noises; *4'33"* asks us to attend to that which we silence (or attempt to silence) in apprehending a work of art. Is this not the same question about willed invisibility that contemporary installations ask of us in an art gallery: where should we stop looking? And has not Marcel Duchamp asked something of the same question in his painting on glass begun in 1915, *The Bride Stripped Bare by Her Bachelors, Even*? Are we to focus on the glass or look through it, and either way, are we to resist the impulse to register the face of the museum visitor staring back at us from the far side of this transparent work of art?

Equating silence and invisibility may allow one to recognize similarities in the aesthetic aims of two very different art forms, but in the end, such a strategy does not bridge those differences for long. If the signifying of silence is more complex than it might seem, at first thought, in literature and music—arts as dependent on silence as on the words and the tones we define as their media—the problem is even more complicated in the visual arts, especially in attempting to distinguish the representation of silence in painting or sculpture or other visual forms from efforts by artists to address silence itself as the subject of their work.

Just as the setting of a poem or a work of fiction may seek to describe a silent scene, the narrative component of a representational painting may evoke the stillness of a place or a moment. A calm pond in a pastoral landscape may suggest an undisturbed quietude, or a fiend poised to pounce upon an unsuspecting victim may give the impression that the whole world is holding its breath in the moment before violence is unleashed. But rather than looking to the representational, one might easily argue that abstract expressionist art, in its refusal to present a recognizable visual image, seems most susceptible to association with silence and most readily lays bare the dilemma of representing an aural phenomenon in a non-audible art form.

A welcoming sign at Houston's Rothko Chapel, for example, announces: "Guests are invited to experience the silence."[8] But whether Mark Rothko's fourteen dark paintings commissioned by Dominique and John de Menil represent silence or merely insist upon it is a question the artist himself, a suicide the year before the chapel opened in 1971, would not have answered. Even as he confessed that he was "interested only in expressing basic human emotions—tragedy, ecstasy, doom, and so on,"[9] he dismissed the notion that paintings could be translated into words, famously explaining, "Silence is so accurate."[10] Perhaps it would be more precise, then, to invite guests to experience that which surpasses language, not silence itself but a form of silence in which language is forced to remain mute.

Similarly, on what basis could we declare Kazimir Malevich's Suprematist painting *Black Square*, his icon of nonrepresentational art, a representation of silence?

He maintained that the 1915 painting depicted nothing, expressed nothing. Yet when he died of cancer in 1935, having spent the last decade of his life producing figurative paintings compatible with the Socialist Realism demanded by Soviet authorities, he lay in state beneath a black square, and mourners at his funeral carried a banner with a black square. Did that icon both represent and protest his silencing? Or was it merely the most famous emblem of the deceased artist, a silent eulogy tolerated by the dictatorship?[11]

It does not take long to recognize, gazing at a work of art, we cannot easily untangle that which represents silence from that which may take silence as its subject. Even more confounding is how easily we confuse silence with that which, by design, merely leaves us speechless. But in proposing that a work of visual art is a silent articulation of human experience, Rothko and Malevich and all those artists who deny language a role in their work elevate silence as a constituent of the medium itself. Just like literature and music, the visual arts are as much a crafting of silence as of the visible materials we assume to be their media.

7 SILENT READING

Just as Laurence Sterne's white page invites the reader to pause, to take refuge from the narrator's words in what might seem an eddy of silence, doesn't every space on a page of writing offer an exit, or even an escape, from the author's voice? But we do not seek refuge in silence when we stop reading; we simply mute the nattering voice that interrupts our own babbling consciousness, or, more generously perhaps, we resolve the duet of two contending voices into our own aria that can scale heights without interruption by, for example, the garrulous Mr. Shandy.

Or by me. Surely the reader has lifted his or her eyes from the pages just read in this very book to consider with no little skepticism the judgments I have asserted about the representation of silence.

Is reading a silent debate, then, one that we enter and from which we constantly withdraw to consider the author's argument and our conclusions about its validity? But not all reading is this kind of duel, a dialogue of thrust and parry. Swept along by a compelling narrative and well-crafted sentences, who has not been lost in another's consciousness only to be startled back into the moment by a ringing phone or some other interruption? And actually wasn't the reading itself the interruption, at least of our own sense of self, and the knock at the door the slap that awakened us from a kind of dream?

Like walkie-talkies that require a button be pressed to speak and released to hear, does reading require that either the voice of the author or the voice of the reader's consciousness be silenced at any given moment? Such an analogy suggests that reading is an act of hospitality toward another's mind, in which we silence our voice in courtesy to the voice of another's consciousness, a voice that alternates with our own in conversation.

But what happens when circumstances demand the complete attention of one's consciousness? Won't the ink on the page remain mute stains unless the reader has the breath to plump them into words and the attention to reinvigorate the thoughts those silent letters preserve? To read, must consciousness be at its leisure to admit the voice of another? Or put another way, will a preoccupied mind refuse to be silenced long enough to read? And so is reading at least an intermittent silencing of the self, a silence intolerable when that self is under threat?

It is said that with the onset of a serious illness the first thing to be lost is the capacity to read. I learned the truth of that insight ten years ago, not from sickness but from homelessness.

Having fled the approach of Hurricane Katrina in 2005, my family and I took refuge in my brother's house in Dallas, expecting to return to New Orleans a day or two later. The storm, with recorded winds in the city under 100 miles per hour and, thus, only a strong category one hurricane, did not destroy New Orleans that August Monday morning. But in its wake, defective levees designed and built by the U.S. Army Corps of Engineers collapsed and flooded 80 percent of the city, an area seven times the size of Manhattan, with saltwater up to fourteen feet deep.

By that Thursday, we were coming to understand we could not return home anytime soon. My sister, also living in the Dallas area, brought us to a film, *The 40-Year-Old Virgin*, to take our minds off the still unfolding catastrophe. As the comedy unspooled in the darkened auditorium, I began to feel as if I couldn't breathe. That night, I told my wife what had happened. She was shocked—because she had experienced the same sense of suffocation. In fact, she told me, she almost had had to leave the theater in the middle of the film.

It had nothing to do with the movie we tried to watch that night; I still have no idea what its plot is. But the experience of engaging imaginatively with the story on the screen was nearly unendurable. In the following weeks, while we waited for martial law to be lifted and the army to allow us to return to our destroyed home, we learned that reading had become just as difficult as watching that film.

We eventually recovered the ability to read and watch films, but only to a limited degree. Before the levee collapse, we would often catch three movies in a single weekend, but even now, ten years later, it's an unusual week when we watch a film. And I still find it impossible to lose myself in a book as I once could.

If I bring up this lasting effect among other New Orleanians who survived the flood and its aftermath, many will admit the same disability—and usually they are relieved to learn that someone else can't read anymore.

I think what happened to us, what can happen to someone seriously ill, is related to the silencing of the self that reading requires. Confronting an array of problems that occur to the victim of disaster or disease only little by little—do I still have a job, what am I going to do for money, will my insurance cover what I'm facing, will my marriage survive this, how is my life going to change—one holds on tightly to the self. One doesn't dare let go.

But reading (or watching a film) requires yielding consciousness to someone else. The inventory of worries that preoccupy one who is struggling to reimagine his or her life can't be put aside, even in sleep. New Orleanians will confess how, in the days following the levee collapse, they would awaken at two or three in the morning, suddenly realizing, for example, that they couldn't access their money because their bank and its computers were underwater. I can confirm from personal experience that one doesn't fall back asleep after such an awakening. One lies wide awake in the dark, eyes open, waiting for dawn, trying not to disturb the person next to you in bed, who probably is awake, too, and lying still in hopes one of you, at least, might sleep through the night.

So I couldn't read. My ability to write, though, was undiminished by the psychological trauma of seeing my hometown destroyed. Returning to the city five weeks after the levee collapses, our house uninhabitable, we slept in a daycare center without hot water, where—seated on a twelve-inch-high blue plastic chair with my portable computer resting on a barely taller red plastic table—I wrote fifteen columns for *The New York Times*.

Undistracted by circumstances, I composed column after column, one of which noted the loss of my personal library and a few examples of the 2,500 books ruined by the water that flooded our house. Readers from around the country began to send me copies of the particular titles I had mentioned as well as their own favorite books: the collected poems of Elizabeth Bishop, a gilt-edged copy of Ralph Waldo Emerson's essays, Robert Fagles's translation of *The Odyssey*. Lovely, heartfelt gifts, but I wasn't able to read them.

If my experience guides, reading is, essentially, a fitful silencing of the self, at least when the self is able to accept silence. But such a formulation necessarily throws into doubt the possibility of truly silent reading, which we take as a form of solitude. Just as we hesitate to interrupt someone at prayer, we excuse ourselves when distracting an individual from silent reading as if intruding upon privacy. But reading is no more solitary than a telephone conversation, and even this notion that reading is a silent or private act is relatively modern.

Early in his *Confessions*, Augustine notes the habit of Ambrose, his teacher, to read silently. Unusual enough in his day for Augustine to spend a paragraph describing and then justifying the practice, he guesses that by so doing, Ambrose wraps himself in a silence his students dare not pierce with questions. Though he goes on to other justifications, such as getting through books more quickly and preserving the voice from hoarseness, in the end Augustine must admit he doesn't know the motive but trusts his teacher has a good reason for doing it.[1]

Augustine's account suggests that reading in antiquity was most commonly a communal activity fostering debate among its listeners. In universities today, so persistent is the influence of this practice that classes are called lectures (whose etymology derives from the Latin *legere*, "to read," and its past participle, *lectus*), and many academic conferences are still structured around the reading aloud of papers. Even more pronounced a tradition in religious communities, most liturgies include readings of scripture to the congregation, and some monasteries continue to furnish their refectories with a lectern for readings during meals.

Roger Chartier traces the emergence of silent reading from medieval copyists to university scholars around the time of the founding of the University of Paris in the middle of the twelfth century. He notes that silent reading had become the norm for educated readers by the fifteenth century but even four hundred years later, *La Cagnotte*, Eugène Marin Labiche's 1864 comedy, mocks a farmer for reading a private letter aloud; the bumpkin retorts that he can't understand what he reads unless he hears it.[2]

The familiar functions of reading aloud are still recognizable, of course, whether it is Samuel Pepys's reading to his wife three nights before Christmas 1667 to distract her from a toothache, or young Jem's reading to Mrs. Dubose as the old woman struggles to overcome her morphine addiction in *To Kill a Mockingbird*, or the old man's reading of *The Princess Bride* to his sick grandson. Clara Claiborne Park recalls in a 1980 essay on the nature of memory that her mother read to her sisters while they sewed and that the father of a college friend read a chapter of Dickens to his family every night at dinner.[3] But the habit of reading aloud to others, except in the home to our youngest children, has faded throughout my lifetime.

For the most part, reading aloud, at least for adults, has ceased to be communal, but there are a few exceptions. Despite the spread of literacy and the elimination of the need for public readings of governmental notices, for example, vestiges of the practice survive in corners of our society. Audio books, a term that would have been a redundancy in earlier times, have a wide contemporary audience, and reading tablets such as the iPad and the Kindle offer a feature that allows the device to read the text aloud when one's eyes have grown weary. Most American fiction writers, and nearly all poets, make more money reading their work to audiences of fans than from the publication of that same work. Some of the popularity of literary readings must be ascribed to the contemporary cult of celebrity—if "celebrity" can be used without guffaws in a description of novelists and poets in the twenty-first century. But a sense of shared interest unites the readers of a particular writer when they gather to hear the work aloud, and one does come away from such a performance with a clearer sense of the rhythm of the author's words. Park reminds us in her essay that, as Moses Hadas has pointed out, for the Greeks literature was "something to be listened to in public rather than scanned silently in private."[4] Literary readings honor that tradition.

But do we actually scan the written word silently? Recent neurological research questions whether silent reading actually is silent. Evidence grows that the brain interprets "silent" reading as an auditory phenomenon.

In "Silent Reading of Direct versus Indirect Speech Activates Voice-selective Areas in the Auditory Cortex," published in *The Journal of Cognitive Neuroscience* in 2011, Bo Yao and his colleagues reported: "Overall, our results lend objective empirical support to the intuitive experience of an 'inner voice' during silent reading of written text, particularly during silent reading of direct speech statements."[5]

The following year, Marcela Perrone-Bertolotti et al., in "How Silent Is Silent Reading? Intracerebral Evidence for Top-Down Activation of Temporal Voice Areas during Reading" in *The Journal of Neuroscience*, explained: "As you might experience it while reading this sentence, silent reading often involves an imagery speech component: we can hear our own 'inner voice' pronouncing words mentally. Recent functional magnetic resonance imaging studies have associated that component with increased metabolic activity in the auditory cortex, including voice-selective areas."[6]

The authors went on to announce experimental confirmation of Yao's findings that "reading spontaneously elicits auditory processing in the absence of any auditory stimulation."[7] Using "direct electrophysiological recordings from the auditory cortex to show that silent reading activates voice-selective regions of the auditory cortex,"[8] they concluded that "written words produce a vivid auditory experience almost effortlessly" and readers "produce inner voice even when reading narrative with no identified speaker."[9] But the authors cautioned that "sustained inner voice activation is not an automatic process occurring systematically in response to any written word. It is clearly enhanced when participants read attentively (to understand and memorize sentences) and minimized when words are not processed attentively."[10]

When we read rather than merely skim a text, the experience is processed as auditory. Silent reading is not silent to the brain—or to most of us.

Perrone-Bertolotti notes, rather offhandedly in the article's introduction, that "few would contest that most of our waking time is spent talking to ourselves covertly."[11] But a 2010 article by Julie Cross in *The Daily Mail* reported on the case of a fifty-year-old dyslexic builder living in Stoke-on-Trent who was amazed to learn that his wife heard a voice in her head when she read silently: "I have never heard a voice in my head—ever. I was so shocked I nearly fell off my chair." He went on to explain: "It all seemed so alien to me. I have the reading age of a five-year-old so I never read. If I dream, I have visual dreams. They are always totally silent." He says the impact on his life has been enormous. "I now understand my actions a lot more. I follow my emotions because I don't have a voice in my head analysing what I'm about to say or do."[12]

Professor Rod Nicolson at the University of Sheffield is pursuing a link between dyslexia and the absence of inner speech. "Everyone assumes everyone else is the same. However, we have found not everyone has an inner voice and in those who don't, literacy levels are often poor. But we have also found a lot of children with dyslexia who have well-developed inner speech." Dr. Kate Saunders, of the British Dyslexia Association, says, according to the article, that "30 to 50 per cent of those with dyslexia also have Attention Deficit Hyperactivity Disorder, a medical condition affecting how well someone can sit still and focus. It is believed that many of those with ADHD may also lack an inner voice."[13]

Inheritance, as well, may play a role: the dyslexic builder has two adult children, both with dyslexia and no internal speech.

So, though there are clearly a number of factors at play in dyslexia, not only is silent reading a misnomer—silence may actually be an impediment to reading.

8 SILENCE ON STAGE

"A juggler doesn't spend the entire performance throwing balls into the air," says Michael Cerveris, the Tony Award-winning actor and singer. "Half the time, the juggler is waiting for the balls to come down."[1]

For Cerveris, the silences in a performance may be more important than the lines delivered. "I really feel grounded in the pauses," he explains. "In those moments, the acting is not diluted by speaking. The silence gives you the opportunity simply to be—and to be silent with the audience."

A major presence in musical theater over the last few decades, Cerveris agrees that rests in musical compositions are not breaks; he particularly embraces the notion that rests are unvoiced notes. In acting, though, another element is at play. "Silences on stage make room for the audience to come to their own conclusions."

Singer and songwriter Paul Simon, in his *New York Times* review of Stephen Sondheim's memoir, *Finishing the Hat*, says something similar about audiences and their need for silences:

> Sondheim quotes the composer-lyricist Craig Carnelia: "True rhyming is a necessity in the theater, as a guide for the ear to know what it has just heard." I have a similar thought regarding attention span and a listener's need for time to digest a complicated line or visualize an unusual image. I try to leave a space after a difficult line—either silence or a lyrical cliché that gives the ear a chance to "catch up" with the song before the next thought arrives and the listener is lost.[2]

But Cerveris sees in stage silences something more than merely a moment to comprehend what was just said: "Silences provide a shared space where the actor and the audience can be quiet together—like a couple that can sit together without speaking. Plays need moments of calm, moments where emotions are shared wordlessly."

So it is not surprising that he sees the management of silences as the performance element most sensitive to the shifting responses of different audiences during a show's run. "One of the most important aspects of rehearsal is pacing and the orchestration of the intermingled silences of the various characters in a play. In performance, the tempos and shapes and durations of silences have to be adjusted every night to respond not just to the audience but also, for example, to another actor sitting in the silences that evening. It can be very frustrating when that happens."

The difference between lines on a page and their presentation on a stage is often the value and variety of silences an experienced actor introduces as he or she translates a script into a performance. Few plays more vigorously test the ability of actors to translate silences on the stage than do those of Harold Pinter. As Peter Hall, former Director of the National Theatre of Great Britain, explains in "Directing Pinter":

> There is a difference in Pinter between a pause and a silence and three dots. A pause is really a bridge where the audience think that you're this side of the river, then when you speak again, you're the other side. That's a pause. And it's alarming, often. It's a gap, which retrospectively gets filled in. It's not a dead stop—that's a silence, where the confrontation has become so extreme, there is nothing to be said until either the temperature has gone down, or the temperature has gone up, and then something quite new happens. Three dots is a very tiny hesitation, but it's there, and it's different from a semicolon, which Pinter almost never uses, and it's different from a comma. A comma is something that you catch up on, you go through it. And a full stop's just a full stop. You stop.[3]

Audiences may not realize how carefully silences of various sorts are inlaid both in the writing and the rehearsal of a play. Even more difficult to distinguish in a performance are the opportunities the playwright provides an actor to adjust silences according to responses of the audience on a particular night. For example, *Shotgun*, the second play in my *Rising Water* trilogy about the flooding of New Orleans and its aftermath, closes its first act with a man's drunken confession to a woman about the death of his wife. In rehearsals for its premiere, Rus Blackwell, a superb actor, urged me to eliminate the questions and exclamations of sympathy his monologue elicits from the character sitting at the kitchen table with him late at night. All that's left of most of those lines of dialogue are the pauses and silences that now punctuate his monologue.[4]

Even less obvious to an audience in such a scene is the artistry of the actor who listens to a long story on stage. During such a monologue, the actor is acting the entire time—though almost entirely in silence. The discipline to stay engaged as the audience fixes attention on the monologuist is one of those elements of the craft of acting that professionals admire but that is nearly invisible to the audience, at least until an unskilled actor demonstrates how difficult it is to remain in silence and in character.

If all that is not complicated enough, Harold Pinter suggests in the introduction to the first volume of his *Complete Works* that even speech can be a form of silence:

There are two silences. One when no word is spoken. The other when perhaps a torrent of language is being employed. This speech is speaking of a language locked beneath it. That is its continual reference. The speech we hear is an indication of that which we don't hear. It is a necessary avoidance, a violent, sly, anguished or mocking smoke screen which keeps the other in its place. When true silence falls we are still left with echo but are nearer nakedness. One way of looking at speech is to say that it is a constant stratagem to cover nakedness.[5]

Of course, such concern with the role of silence on the stage doesn't begin with Pinter. As Leslie Kane points out, "It is not until we come to [Maurice] Maeterlinck that the unexpressed—the eloquent use of silence and unpretentious dialogue implying more than it superficially communicates—'constitutes the main preoccupation of the dramatist.'"[6] Maeterlinck himself explains in his essay "*Le Silence*" that any effort to speak of the most profound of human experiences—death or love, for example—must leave unsaid the truth we don't know how to put into words. Yet in our halting failure to find the words, in our stumbling silences, that truth is glimpsed.[7]

Many commentators contend that the unmooring of belief, of certitude, led to the devaluing of language and the aesthetic elevation of silence in the nineteenth century, as writers increasingly doubted their authority to assert truths. But one might consider whether language itself is yet another of the institutions that came under scrutiny in the period— whether through Ferdinand de Saussure's critical analysis of its structures or Lewis Carroll's whimsical mockery of its arbitrariness. Its authority diminished, language became a medium of faithless practitioners. As Susan Sontag argues, "Confounded by the treachery of words," the modern writer turned to "the pursuit of silence."[8]

Some have been quite literal in that pursuit. In "Is the Playwright Dead?" Lyn Gardner recounts a conversation with Scott Graham of Frantic Assembly, who "talked eloquently about working with Bryony Lavery on *Stockholm* and how she expressed the wish to write silence, condensing a scene to the point where 'words were redundant.'"[9] The Austrian playwright Peter Handke has done just that in *The Hour We Knew Nothing of Each Other*, a hundred-minute play without any words at all.

Nowhere has the pursuit of silence in its multiplicity of forms been more audible than on the modern stage. But there is also another literary silence of the recent past that descends to us in the form of the unspeakable.

9 THE UNSPEAKABLE

Many are familiar with Theodor Adorno's often quoted injunction in the conclusion of his 1949 essay "Cultural Criticism and Society" that silence is the only fitting aesthetic response to the Holocaust: "To write poetry after Auschwitz is barbaric."[1] But fewer know Adorno's later renunciation—or, at least, revision—of his demand that poets should not attempt to speak of the unspeakable:

Perennial suffering has as much right to expression as a tortured man has to scream; hence it may have been wrong to say that after Auschwitz you could no longer write poems. But it is not wrong to raise the less cultural question whether after Auschwitz you can go on living—especially whether one who escaped by accident, one who by rights should have been killed, may go on living. His mere survival calls for the coldness, the basic principle of bourgeois subjectivity, without which there could have been no Auschwitz; this is the drastic guilt of him who was spared. By way of atonement he will be plagued by dreams such as that he is no longer living at all, that he was sent to the ovens in 1944 and his whole existence since has been imaginary, an emanation of the insane wish of a man killed twenty years earlier.[2]

I understand Adorno's initial impulse to forbid poetry to the rest of us. The surviving victim of a man-made catastrophe that obliterated the world he or she had inhabited, perhaps since birth, has lived through so traumatic an experience as to leave one unable to look up from the devastation. The grief and indignation and, yes, unreasoning guilt of the survivor demands acknowledgment and reparation. The laughter of others somewhere else is an affront; their indifference, intolerable.

And I admire the wisdom seventeen years later of his renunciation of the demand for silence, based upon his compassion for others: "Perennial suffering has as much right to expression as a tortured man has to scream."

Such perennial suffering most often finds its genesis in forms of silence. If we begin with the Holocaust itself, was not its intent the silencing of its victims, whether Jews or Roma or homosexuals or some other detested minority? Is that not the point of a genocide (or of its recent euphemism, ethnic cleansing)? A genocide's silencing is, of course, absolute in seeking to erase all traces of the victims, so it does not surprise that book-burning, a silencing bonfire, is often one of its early manifestations—as is state censorship, which systematically silences dissenting voices.

The suppression of dissent through the modern practice of "disappearing" the opposition is yet another application of silence in erasing both political arguments and the individuals who espouse them. The perennial suffering it engenders is caused not only by the loss of loved ones but also by the uncertainty of their fate, for a mystery is, by nature, a silence that persists. The use of silence to prolong the effects of violence, whether indirectly through formal denials that anything has occurred, or more commonly through simply refusing to address the subject, is widely employed by both governments and individuals. For example, the terrorist's refusal to claim responsibility after a bombing or other forms of mass murder seeks to amplify the fear aroused by the violent act through implacable silence, extending the terror generated at least as long as the mystery of its perpetrators remains unsolved.

All such perennial suffering has as much claim to expression, according to Adorno, "as a tortured man has to scream." But there is a difference between genocide and torture. Genocide seeks to silence; torture is the antidote of silence. For what is the purpose of torture (or, to use the American euphemism, enhanced interrogation techniques)? Is it not to force stubborn silence into speech?

Whether we examine medieval judicial proceedings that employed torture to extract a confession (the "Queen of Proofs"), the Inquisition's assault on heresies, or enhanced interrogation techniques applied at Abu Ghraib, the purpose was to coerce information from the silent. The point of torture is not punishment, although torture provides the evidence that will be used later to justify punishment. Nor is the point of torture even pain, which is simply one of the torturer's tools, along with other forms of discomfort, psychological manipulation, and disorientation. The primary purpose of torture is to breach the silence of the individual tortured.

Adorno makes us consider whether the unspeakable demands our silence. But whatever conclusion we draw about that complicated question, it is difficult to dispute that, in the application of violence by the state in defense of its power, the unspeakable nearly always has something to do with silence in one form or another.

IV

10 THE SILENCED MOMENT

A camera is a silencer: the photograph is a glimpse of the world with all the sound leached out. Yes, in a cropped image of an arm, we go on to imagine its hand, and so we fill in the photograph's silence with the chatter, the chirping birdsong, the distant motors, the riffling breeze that our mind insists upon for us to make sense of the puddles of colors, the variegated shadows staining the white paper as, somehow, a fragment of the lived moment. But unlike light, sound does not leave its imprint on the photograph.

In Henri Cartier-Bresson's "Dessau," for example, an enraged Belgian woman, freed from a concentration camp, denounces a Gestapo informer "before she could hide in the crowd," according to Cartier-Bresson's notes. The man seated at the desk in the photograph, taken in April 1945 in Dessau, Germany, may himself have been an inmate of the liberated concentration camp; pen in hand above a pad of paper, he is the only one in the photograph wearing glasses. Behind the accused informer, a man still wearing the striped shirt and pants of the concentration camp stands, arms akimbo. The large crowd filling the frame strains to see the confrontation. In another note, Cartier-Bresson explains the scene in further detail: "Dessau, Germany, 1945. In a camp of displaced persons waiting for repatriation, a Gestapo informer who had pretended to be a refugee is discovered and exposed by a camp inmate whose face is illuminated by the strong, sharp light of rage."[1]

Imagine the furious French words spitting from the mouth of the accuser, the mumbled denial of the accused, the murmur that runs through the crowd. But one man at the back of that crowd, standing on something to see what is happening, looks away to his left; has a sound caught his ear? We cannot tell, for the camera has tweezed out every sound from that moment.

Cartier-Bresson is, of course, not deaf to the silence he creates through his photographs. As he notes in *The Mind's Eye*, "If, in making a portrait, you hope to grasp the interior silence of a willing victim, it's very difficult, but you must somehow position the camera between his shirt and his skin. Whereas with pencil drawing, it is up to the artist to have an interior silence."[2] So a photograph is a distillation of the subject's silence while a drawing is the imposition of the artist's silence.

A photograph is a dialectic of absence and presence. The silence that stains the scene confirms the absence of the photograph's subjects even as it preserves, much like amber hardening around a wasp, the moment in which they lived.

A photograph is, of course, only the veneer of time, skimmed from its flowing surface. Still, who can help but confuse the real and its simulacrum? As Roland Barthes explains, "Whatever it grants to vision and whatever its manner, a photograph is always invisible: it is not it that we see."[3] If we counterpose Michael Polanyi's definition that "Art appears to consist . . . in representing a subject within an artificial framework that contradicts its representative aspects,"[4] we have to question whether a photograph can be construed as a work of art. On the other hand, could we argue that the absence of sound is the "artificial framework" of the photograph?

Here is Barthes again:

A specific photograph, in effect, is never distinguished from its referent (from what it represents), or at least it is not immediately or generally distinguished from its referent (as is the case for every other image, encumbered—from the start, and because of its status— by the way in which the object is simulated). . . . By nature, the Photograph (for convenience's sake, let us accept this universal, which for the moment refers only to the tireless repetition of contingency) has something tautological about it: a pipe, here, is always and intractably a pipe. It is as if the Photograph always carries its referent with itself. . . . The Photograph belongs to that class of laminated objects whose two leaves cannot be separated without destroying them both.[5]

Perhaps that is why we do not recognize the all-encompassing silence of the photograph as silence. We can't hear its absence because we take the photograph for the thing photographed.

Beaumont Newhall suggests that the sadness old snapshots engender have to do with the nature of the medium itself: "The fundamental belief in the authenticity of photographs explains why photographs of people no longer living and of vanished architecture are so melancholy."[6] Like a ghost, they are both absent and present.

Newhall is right: Is there anything more melancholy than silent family films, especially those eight-millimeter reels from the last century? Are the shadows cast on the white screen by a ratcheting projector something other than mute ghosts? Their greetings, their happy banter, do not reach our ears. We watch them silently burst with raucous laughter not knowing—as we do—how the future will wrench sobs from them soon enough.

11 THE SILENCE OF DOLLS

Rainer Maria Rilke, one of Germany's greatest poets, was among the many modern writers who lamented the inability of language to plumb the silence at the core of being: "Oh, how often one longs to speak a few degrees more deeply! My prose . . . lies deeper . . . but one gets only a minimal layer further down; one's left with a mere intimation of the kind of speech that may be possible *there* where silence reigns." One of his efforts "to speak a few degrees more deeply" is "Some Reflections on Dolls," an essay on the wax figurines of Lotte Pritzel. In it, he sketches the uncanny (and melancholy) aspects of the toy most associated with childhood, and in so doing, he reveals the terrible lesson we are taught by the silence of our dolls:

> I wish I could remember if we inveighed against it, flew into a passion and let the monster know that our patience was at an end? If, standing in front of it and trembling with rage, we did not demand to know, item by item,

what actual use it was making of all these riches. It was silent then, not deliberately, it was silent because that was its constant mode of evasion, because it was made of useless and entirely irresponsible material, was silent, and the idea did not occur to it to take some credit to itself on that score, although it could not but gain great importance thereby in a world in which Destiny, and even God Himself, have become famous above all because they answer us with silence. At a time when everyone was still intent on giving us a quick and reassuring answer, the doll was the first to inflict on us that tremendous silence (larger than life) which was later to come to us repeatedly out of space, whenever we approached the frontiers of our existence at any point. It was facing the doll, as it stared at us, that we experienced for the first time (or am I mistaken?) that emptiness of feeling, that heart-pause, in which we should perish did not the whole, gently persisting Nature then lift us across abysses like some lifeless thing. Are we not strange creatures to let ourselves go and to be induced to place our earliest affections where they remain hopeless? So that everywhere there was imparted to that most spontaneous tenderness the bitterness of knowing that it was in vain? Who knows if such memories have not caused many a man afterwards, out there in life, to suspect that he is not lovable?[1]

As dolls silently regard us, their fixed expressions offering no hint of their judgments about what passes before their glass eyes, an inexorable indifference rebuffs our entreaties. And so we learn that indifference, too, in its refusal to acknowledge us, or our desires, is a form of silence. But that is not the only lesson about silence in which we are tutored by dolls.

Is a doll not a kind of mirror of the child—or at least a reflection of what the child knows itself once to have been? And as that past is cradled in small arms, cooed over, perhaps even lullabied by a little girl's artless voice, how does the doll respond to such unrestrained affection? With silence, of course. Yes, we may dissect the past as if it were a poem to be explicated, excavate the buried memory, interrogate the record, but it is not the past that answers our questions. In the face of silence, we impose what we take for answers. We are, at best, ventriloquists, and the past, our dummy. For no matter how articulately we phrase those questions we ask of what—of who—we once were, our past remains mute as the doll in a child's embrace.

Children, of course, find nothing unsettling in the dolls we bestow upon them as gifts. Only we adults, straying into a nursery, are disturbed by the silent visages of dolls plumped like pillows against the headboard of a narrow bed too small for our grown bodies. What once was familiar, even intimate, now appears to us as something foreign, even ominous.

In his 1919 essay on "The Uncanny," Sigmund Freud traces the etymology of *heimlich* and *unheimlich* (the homey or cozy and the uncanny) in order to understand what the uncanny might have to do with the familiar. Freud follows this etymological study with a psychoanalytical reading of E. T. A. Hoffmann's "The Sandman," a story about the hopeless love of a student for a neighbor's daughter, Olympia. The boy's beloved is eventually exposed as merely an animated doll, an automaton ("For the first time now he saw her exquisitely formed face. Only her eyes seemed peculiarly fixed and lifeless")[2]; the shock of this revelation is tangled with forgotten childhood fears that resume their hold on the student. Freud explains Hoffmann's logic:

> The frightening element is something that has been repressed and now returns. This species of the frightening would then constitute the uncanny, and it would be immaterial whether it was itself originally frightening or arose from another affect. In the second place, if this really is the secret nature of the uncanny, we can understand why German usage allows the familiar (*das Heimliche*, the "homely") to switch to its opposite, the uncanny (*das Unheimliche*, the "unhomely"), for this uncanny element is actually nothing new or strange, but something that was long familiar to the psyche and was estranged from it only through being repressed. The link with repression now illuminates Schelling's definition of the uncanny as "something that should have remained hidden and has come into the open."[3]

Having gone on to review the consequences of this insight, Freud concludes the essay, almost offhandedly, with an extraordinary assertion: "As for solitude, silence and darkness, all we can say is that these are factors connected with infantile anxiety, something that most of us never wholly overcome."[4]

If Freud is correct that the familiar, repressed, returns as the uncanny, what is it about the doll that we repress? Certainly its silence. Children, after all, do not think of dolls as silent. The domestic scenes a child reenacts in a playroom, the classes she conducts for her dolls propped against a toy chest, the doctor's visit in which a doll is questioned about its health complaints by an eight-year-old—these improvised theatricals all appear to feature dialogue although the audience can hear only a single actor. Such child's play with a doll finds its parallel in poetry's dramatic monologue, in which an auditor, whose lines of dialogue are never included but prompt responses from the speaker, silently inhabits the poem. Similarly, when we overhear a little girl arguing with her doll about some mischief, it is only the child's monologue we hear.

So children never seem to realize that dolls—apart, perhaps, from those that bleat a startled "Mama" if squeezed violently enough—are silent. Nor does Nathanael, Hoffmann's student who falls in love with a doll. Though the automaton he adores can produce only shrill songs and mechanical sighs, he defends his beloved's silence: "I discover myself again only in Olympia's love. That she does not indulge in jabbering banalities like other shallow people may not seem right to you. It's true that she says little; but the few words she does utter are in a sacred language which expresses an inner world imbued with love."[5] He goes on to insist, "What are words? Mere words! The glance of her heavenly eyes expresses more than any commonplace speech."[6] Having earlier dismissed his flesh-and-blood fiancée as a "damned, lifeless automaton"[7] after she had criticized his poetry, he detects no criticism in Olympia's eyes but only "the yearning glance with which she looked at him."[8] Unfortunately for the young man, his mistake is brutally revealed: "Nathanael stood transfixed; he had only too clearly seen that in the deathly pale waxen face of Olympia there were no eyes, but merely black holes. She was a lifeless doll."[9] Childlike in asserting a willful reading of her silence as eloquent affirmation of his desire to be loved without reservation, Nathanael is, in the end, driven mad by everything his delusion has forced him to repress. But perhaps that repression is a symptom of adulthood, not childhood.

Walter Benjamin posits that children are not like us. What we take for innocence may be sheer savagery, and so what is familiar to a child—that a doll is a kind of silent corpse, for example, completely at the mercy of the living—we repress in adulthood until the dead eyes of an abandoned toy fix us with its unblinking stare.

It took a long time before people realized, let alone incorporated the idea into dolls, that children are not just men and women on a reduced scale. It is well known that even children's clothing became emancipated from that of adults only at a very late date. Not until the nineteenth century, in fact. It sometimes looks as if our century wishes to take this development one step further and, far from regarding children as little men and women, has reservations about thinking of them as human beings at all. People have now discovered the grotesque, cruel, grim side of children's life. While meek and mild educators still cling to Rousseauesque dreams, writers like Ringelnatz and painters like Klee have grasped the despotic and dehumanized element in children. Children are insolent and remote from the world. After all the sentimentality of a revived Biedermeier, Mynona is probably right in his views of 1916: ". . . My children would not like to be without their guillotines and gallows, at the very least."[10]

The association of the silent doll and the voiceless corpse is nowhere more explicit than in the creation of one of the world's most famous dolls, one quite literally conceived beneath "guillotines and gallows." Marina Warner recounts the grisly tale in *Phantasmagoria: Spirit Visions, Metaphors, and Media into the Twenty-first Century*:

The oldest surviving waxwork in Madame Tussaud's in London is called "The Sleeping Beauty": a female figure lying down, in the kind of pose often called abandoned; as if spellbound rather than asleep, she seems suspended for all eternity like an effigy on a tomb awaiting the resurrection, her relaxed, even languorous slumber a wishful fiction about death's defeat. The figure's face is hard to see, unless you go around her to look at her upside down—and then the upturned angle offers her throat and breast to the spectator's attention before anything else. This is indeed the most spectacular aspect of her: her breast rises and falls to her breathing. She looks alive. She looks real. She looks as if she has overcome time and death; she creates an illusion of life to strike wonder in the beholder.[11]

Warner goes on to explain the history of "The Sleeping Beauty," modeled in 1765 on the 22-year-old Marie Jean du Barry, the mistress of Louis XV, by the Swiss physician and wax sculptor Philippe Curtius, who became the mentor of Marie Tussaud. As late as 1995, Madame Tussaud's Wax Museum insisted "The Sleeping Beauty" was, in fact, Curtius's wax sculpture of Madame du Barry, though enhanced at the beginning of the twentieth century with an electrified clockwork breast. (The young woman's waxen face was said to be not du Barry's but that of the lovely and virtuous Madame de Saint Amaranthe, who was condemned to the guillotine after rejecting Robespierre's advances.) Nearly executed herself during the Reign of Terror in the aftermath of the French Revolution, Tussaud found employment casting death masks of such notables as Louis XVI, Marie Antoinette, Marat, and even Robespierre himself.[12]

By the time Tussaud exhibited her work in London in 1802, her collection included two more "Sleeping Beauties."

As Warner notes, "In the other two cases of the recumbent figures, Curtius or Marie modelled their likenesses from . . . severed heads: a contemporary who claimed to be an eyewitness described how in the cemetery of La Madeleine, Curtius rearranged Du Barry's rictus with a deft pinch of his finger and thumb: '*Il maquilla cette face d'un sourire posthume, la fit belle et agréable*' ('He made up the face with a posthumous smile, rendered her beautiful and charming'— Du Barry was one of the few victims who had gone to her death protesting violently). He then poured a layer of wax straight on to the turf at the side of the grave, and rolled the severed head in it to take an impression of her features."[13]

Mixing sleep and death, like a drugged Juliet awaiting her Romeo, "The Sleeping Beauty" is a life-sized doll, a doll that betrays the familiar figure of a beautiful sleeping woman with the terrible repressed truth of a corpse's face pinched into a smile and rouged to conceal the gray wax of her cheeks.

In "Tailors' Dummies," Bruno Schulz offers a frightening aside in his story about a man's father lecturing seamstresses at work beside a dressmaker's mannequin: "Have you heard at night the terrible howling of these wax figures, shut in the fair-booths; the pitiful chorus of those forms of wood or porcelain, banging their fists against the walls of their prisons?"[14] The ghastly history of "The Sleeping Beauty" almost convinces us that, alone in the dark waxwork museum, perhaps the young woman does cry out in her sleep in the midst of the terrifying nightmare she has endured for over two centuries.

But, no, more terrible than her howl at midnight is her perpetual silence, even as her chest rises and falls.

A ghoulish parallel to the interchangeable head of "The Sleeping Beauty" can be found in *Ozma of Oz*, the third novel in L. Frank Baum's Oz series for children, in which Dorothy is taken prisoner by the headless Princess Langwidere:

> Now I must explain to you that the Princess Langwidere had thirty heads—as many as there are days in the month. But of course she could only wear one of them at a time, because she had but one neck. These heads were kept in what she called her "cabinet," which was a beautiful dressing-room that lay just between Langwidere's sleeping-chamber and the mirrored sitting-room. Each head was in a separate cupboard lined with velvet. The cupboards ran all around the sides of the dressing-room, and had elaborately carved doors with gold numbers on the outside and jeweled-framed mirrors on the inside of them.
>
> When the Princess got out of her crystal bed in the morning she went to her cabinet, opened one of the velvet-lined cupboards, and took the head it contained from its golden shelf. Then, by the aid of the mirror inside the open door, she put on the head—as neat and straight as could be—and afterward called her maids to robe her for the day.[15]

As Benjamin argues, children are amused to exercise mastery over the helpless, long-suffering doll, as we seem to be as we savor the wax sculpture of the silent, sleeping female. But the child knows there is more pleasure in tormenting something that can complain. That screech of pain distinguishes a pet from a doll, as Charles Baudelaire explains in "The Philosophy of Toys":

On a main road, behind the wrought-iron grille of a fine garden at the far end of which gleamed a handsome château, stood a handsome and blooming little boy, dressed in one of those country outfits that are so full of coquetry. Luxury, freedom from cares, and the daily spectacle of wealth have so prettified these children as to make them seem a different species from those born and bred in mediocrity and poverty. Beside him a magnificent doll lay on the ground, looking as neat and clean as its master, varnished and gilded, dressed in a beautiful tunic, covered in feathers and glass beads. But the child was paying no attention to his toy. This is what he was looking at: on the other side of the grille, on the road, among the thistles and nettles stood another boy, dirty, somewhat rickety, one of those urchins along whose cheeks the snot slowly winds a path through the dust and grime. Between those symbolic bars of iron, the poor child was showing his toy to the rich child, who was examining it greedily, as a rare and unknown object. And this toy, which the little brat was tormenting and shaking up and down in its makeshift cage, was a live rat.[16]

Adults, of course, do not play with dolls. Rather, they don masks and become dolls themselves. And the silence of the mask strapped to a human face is far more fearsome than the stillness of the doll. For what do we make of a man refashioned by a carnival costume into a doll—sheathed in motley, the head jingling in its cap and bells, the impassive mask as unflinching as a porcelain face, and the eyes, those still-human eyes, regarding us with secret mirth?

Is any contradiction more chilling than human eyes behind masks mocking human faces? And what dreadful lessons can we draw from the implacable silence of masks? Whom do we recognize in the silent indifference of the masked reveler but ourselves? The emotionless mask mirrors the dread that, within each of us, skulks a sociopath, unmoved by the suffering of others and attentive only to our own interests. Of course, we never speak of this possibility; repression, too, is a form of silence.

So one can understand the revulsion of some cultures at graven images and may wonder at our Western nonchalance in their presence. A statue, or any image, for that matter, is—what?—a hardened shadow, a congealed memory. Why shouldn't dolls worry us with their rouged lips pursed in a perpetual pout, their miniature wigs of women's curls knotted into their perforated porcelain skulls, their fragile china hands and feet fastened by twine to muslin arms and legs stuffed with straw? Who should apologize for uneasiness in the presence of such a homunculus? For despite the horrible weighted eyelids that flick open and shut at every jolt, the doll is more corpse than quick. Yet we call it a toy, forcing it on our children.

Of course, in the end, nearly every doll is actually a silent victim we bend to our will, whether the mouthless effigy of a despised politician we burn in a town square, uncomplaining toy soldiers we topple on tabletop battlefields, the speechless golem of Judaic legend tasked as a servant, or the rag doll we leave to the mercy of a child's whims.

This fundamental truth about the silence of dolls is nowhere more nakedly asserted than in Hans Bellmer's series of photographs of his sculptures published as *The Doll* in 1934 and similar work he created throughout that decade. Bellmer cited a performance of Jacques Offenbach's opera *The Tales of Hoffmann*—whose first act is based on "The Sandman" and the doomed love of the hero for Olympia, the automaton—as one of the inspirations for his disturbing life-sized nude dolls, grotesque assemblages of dismembered heads and torsos and ball-joints and limbs, twisted into sexually explicit poses and presented as convulsive monstrosities.[17] Always female and displayed in the haphazard posture of a sprawled corpse, Bellmer's dolls, legs splayed and often clothed only in a schoolgirl's white socks and black shoes, are, as Robert Hughes wrote, "almost infinitely pornographic."[18] Never protesting the contortions and amputations and deformities they endure, the dolls are perfect victims: unresisting and silent.

And yet we fear them.

12 SILENCING

In our first visit to Florence, while still students, my wife and I found a little restaurant near our bat-infested *pensione* as sunset turned the Arno bronze. Having been raised by her grandmother from Viareggio, the nearby beach resort, Marsha ordered our meal in an Italian our old waiter would have recognized as native to Tuscany. He, however, refused to write anything on his pad until impatiently interrupting her with a stern "*Signorina!*" he turned to me inquisitively. Only after I nodded did he scribble down our order.

Later, trying to master the craft of teaching, I read an article about the tendency of both male and female teachers to interrupt female—but not male—students when answering questions. Of course, I thought myself exempt from such sexism until I began to make an effort to restrain myself from interrupting students. It quickly became obvious to me that I had to remind myself to allow the student to complete an answer when that student was a woman but I had few occasions to practice such restraint when a man was speaking in the class. I found myself rarely on the verge of interruption if the student was male.

There was little comfort to be drawn from the research that indicated I would have been just as likely to interrupt a female student if I had been female myself. I found even more troubling than this revelation about my teaching the recognition that my female students had endured an education their whole lives in which instructors cut short their insights while their male classmates were accorded full attention. It's impossible to believe that such behavior by teachers and other respected authority figures would not have lifelong consequences for those silenced through interruptions as well as through less obvious pressures to defer to the judgments of male counterparts.

We live in a world where women are often silenced, sometimes violently. But the daily indignity of being casually silenced is so much a part of a woman's experience that such less dramatic instances of the imposition of silence on another human being, as a waiter's or a teacher's curt interruption, may actually illuminate more fully than draconian examples the role of silence in maintaining existing distributions of power in society. Silenced myself by the limitations a small book imposes upon its author, I offer only a single example, though volumes remain to be written about the silencing not only of women but of all those marginalized by the speech of the powerful.

Bessie Dendrinos and Emilia Ribeiro Pedro demonstrate how much is to be gleaned from analysis of an easily overlooked silencing of women in daily life: the giving of street directions.[1] In their review of the literature about silence and gender, the researchers reference an earlier study whose author "presents data which show how men exercised power in their daily communicative encounters with their female partners by being silent. The relatively silent behavior of husbands tended to silence their wives, who thus worked harder to maintain the interaction but whose efforts were confounded by their partners' frequent 'no-response' turn-taking violations." Dendrinos and Pedro note both that "Power is routinely exercised through speech" and that "Power . . . may also be exercised through silence."

At the highest levels of authority, the latter may be preferred. In *Le Fil de l'épée*, his 1932 meditation on leadership, Charles de Gaulle writes, "*Rien ne rehausse l'autorité mieux que le silence, splendeur des forts et refuge des faibles.*" His perhaps surprising insight loses little in translation: "Nothing enhances authority better than silence, splendor of the strong and refuge of the weak."[2] But de Gaulle goes further: "Silence is the ultimate weapon of power."[3] Part of his meaning surely lies in George Bernard Shaw's line in *Back to Methuselah* (1921) that "Silence is the most perfect expression of scorn."[4] But more than that, the questions of the powerless, the demands of the dispossessed, can be ignored by the powerful with impunity. Leonardo da Vinci agrees: "Nothing strengthens authority so much as silence."[5] (Of course, one could read that to mean that the silence of the ruled strengthens the ruler. On the other hand, da Vinci, always at the mercy of powerful patrons, was well acquainted with agonizingly long waits for a ruler to break his silence and authorize a new commission.)

In giving street directions, though, he who speaks seems to assert authority. The researchers based their conclusions on thirty-four random instances of a female asking for directions from various groups in cities and smaller towns in Portugal and Greece; they found no significant differences in the responses elicited in the two countries.

Some interesting gender-specific details emerged. When women couldn't provide directions, they apologized; men didn't. Women used "will" in giving directions; men used "must." Men also tended to use repetition. But the role of silence in giving directions was the element most clearly gender specific.

For example, in the few instances in which a pair of women were asked for directions, "the role of informant seemed to be negotiated" by eye contact. Groups of men, on the other hand, spoke over one another until one emerged to give directions. But in nearly all mixed-sex groups, "it was the males that ultimately assumed the role of informant." The women present were either silent throughout or silenced. When women began to provide directions, they eventually "gave up their role as informants. In only one encounter, when the man had completed his turn, the woman confirmed what her companion had said, and repeated his last utterance verbatim." In other encounters, females who could have corrected the inaccurate directions provided by a male either remained silent or, rather than directly correcting him, asked a question that would make him rethink the directions.

A particularly interesting exchange occurred when directions were asked of a small group of thirty- to forty-year-old men:

> One of the men responded immediately and proceeded, without any interruption from the others, to give long and complicated directions. A woman in her twenties, coming out of a nearby bakery, heard the confusing explanation and intervened to help clarify the man's account. But as soon as she began to talk, she was interrupted by the same man who had spoken and who now began to repeat what he had said before. The woman intervened again and was allowed to complete her turn of short and precise directions. At that moment, another man who had witnessed the whole incident took the floor and spoke in a loud and authoritative tone, as if to correct the female speaker. However, he simply paraphrased the information which had been provided by the woman.

In the only two instances in the research where women were allowed to provide directions, men still had the last word. The example that brought to mind our dinner in Florence nearly half a century ago involved another young couple. After the woman had offered her two sentences of simple directions, "her male companion looked at us and confirmed: '*Sosta*. That's right.'"

The old waiter who upbraided Marsha that summer evening long ago would have approved of the young man.

13 SILENCE AND SECRETS

Unknown until discovered among the papers of a British aristocrat in 1911, *Silence* is a thirteenth-century French romance. The introduction to a recent translation summarizes the surprising tale:

> The plot, reduced to a minimum, is that Silence, the daughter of Cador and Eufemie of Cornwall, is raised as a boy because Eban, king of England, will not allow women to inherit. When she reaches adolescence, Nature and Nurture appear as vituperative allegorical figures who torment her. Reason tells her to continue her life as a male. She runs away to learn the art of minstrelsy and then becomes a famous knight. Having repeatedly rejected the advances of Eban's highly sexed wife, Eufeme (who fakes a bloody rape attempt), Silence is sent on a supposedly hopeless quest: the capture of Merlin, who has prophesied that he can be taken only by a woman's trick. She succeeds, but is unmasked by Merlin, as is the

queen and the queen's latest lover, disguised as a nun. Justice is done, women's right to inherit is restored, and Silence becomes queen of England through marriage with Eban.[1]

A secret is at the heart of *Silence*, and in naming its heroine Silence the romance's author acknowledges that a secret is a form of silence. Guarded by the initiated, a secret segregates—or even hoards—knowledge. We recognize its power almost instinctively, begging to be admitted to its inner sanctum, walled round with silence. Hungry for the forbidden, we press for details. Denied, we may come to resent the authority of those who conceal knowledge from us.

Such a response is an expression of modern individualism; a traditional society, on the other hand, accepts the need for that which may not be known by all, that which may not be spoken by any, that which must be veiled in silence.

In its own way, *Silence* is reminiscent of the contemporary (and perhaps centuries-old) Afghan practice of *bacha posh*, literally "dressed up as a boy," in which a daughter is selected to be raised as a son. Like the character Silence, as Jenny Nordberg explains, most such children eventually return to womanhood, and as in the case of Silence, the purpose is practical:

> In a land where sons are more highly valued, since in the tribal culture usually only they can inherit the father's wealth and pass down a name, families without boys are

the objects of pity and contempt. Even a made-up son increases the family's standing, at least for a few years. A *bacha posh* can also more easily receive an education, work outside the home, even escort her sisters in public, allowing freedoms that are unheard of for girls in a society that strictly segregates men and women.[2]

A traditional society, especially if relatively isolated, may be able to sustain an institution dependent upon secrecy like that of the *bacha posh*, but the modern world, having squandered so many other kinds of silences, now amuses itself by exposing secrets—whether in the form of celebrity scandals, humiliating reality shows, pornography, or political exposés.

The consequences of living in a world without curtains may be as serious as the daily price paid for living in a world without silence.

In the wake of the disclosure of a secret American surveillance program by Edward Snowden, a National Security Agency contractor, the *Financial Times* published a commentary by John Thornhill. He begins by conceding the misdeeds of governments, British parliamentarians, the police, and even the press: "Can you trust the press, which revels in exposing the shortcomings of other institutions? It has itself been condemned for blurring journalism and activism. . . . Politicians are asking who has given newspaper editors—and their semi-detached journalists—the authority to decide what is—and is not—harmful to the state's interests?" The history of the United States during my lifetime has been punctuated by betrayals of public trust by those in positions of authority: the Pentagon Papers, the Watergate scandal, Iran-Contra, the shuffling of pedophile priests from parish to parish by Catholic bishops. In my experience, secrets (and the silence that is the mask of secrets) have been employed by the powerful to conceal falsehoods and crimes. But Thornhill points out what increasing transparency has cost us:

> Idealists may lament this crisis of trust in our institutions and argue for a more honest debate. Some demand more transparency and accountability. Yet Onora O'Neill, the philosopher, has questioned whether these are the best remedies for restoring trust. In brilliant Reith lectures, given more than a decade ago, she argued that public distrust had grown in the very years in which transparency and accountability had been so avidly pursued. The information revolution may be anti-authoritarian but it can also be anti-democratic. "Transparency and openness may not be the unconditional goods that they are fashionably supposed to be. By the same token, secrecy and lack of transparency may not be the enemies of trust," she said.[3]

In a talk I gave at a writers' conference during the Clinton impeachment hearings, I wondered about the effect of local newspapers around the country discussing in print whether fellatio constituted "sexual relations." I admitted that conservatives were surely scoring political points by exposing in salacious detail the affair of the President with a young woman, but I worried that introducing such topics into the nation's public discourse must further the coarsening of our culture that they had professed to abhor and for which they continued to blame liberals. Once the private becomes public, I argued, it can never recover the silence that society has previously accorded it through social conventions protecting the personal against public exposure.

I was reminded of that talk a decade or so later when the PEN/Faulkner Foundation asked me to speak at a New Orleans high school that had been rebuilt after the levee collapses of 2005. The organization had supplied copies of my novel, *Oyster*, to the students and their teachers in advance of my visit. Set in Plaquemines Parish in 1957, *Oyster* recounts a feud between two families over oyster leases as oil companies cut canals through the marshes of Louisiana, destroying both the wetlands and the oyster reefs that had flourished there for centuries.

I had expected the students to ask questions about the transformation of the role of women, which the novel traces over four generations, or the violence that propels much of the action. Instead, students expressed shock at the secrets that threaded through every aspect of life in a remote small town fifty years ago. One student said she found the secrets adults concealed from members of their own family more frightening than any of the murders I described.

Standing there, I realized they had grown up in a world without secrets. No subject had been hidden from them; no language, forbidden; no knowledge, postponed. So the notion that some people concealed the most important, the most intimate, the most shocking experiences of their lives, rather than sharing such stories with family members or on social media or through some other public forum, unsettled the students.

How different a world they inhabited from the one in which my mother and her sisters would switch to Italian for family matters meant to be kept secret from us children (though thanks to a bit of schoolboy Latin, I wasn't entirely surprised when my Aunt Jean left my Uncle Joe).

Where nothing goes unsaid, talk never stops. Silence is banished along with the secrets it guarded. But even as more and more kinds of secrets wither under public scrutiny, one form of secrecy is, thanks to the Internet, more widely employed today than at any previous time.

Onora O'Neill addressed this other intersection of the secret and the silent in a 2013 interview with Josh Booth about, among other things, the regulation of anonymity on the Internet. The author of an anonymous posting is, of course, a secret; to write anonymously is—playing a bit with a term developed by Martin Heidegger and Jacques Derrida—to write under erasure. And erasures, like lacunae, are moments of silence in a text. If, when we seek the author's name, we are answered with silence, it is not difficult to define anonymity not only as a secret but also as a silence. Though she recognizes instances in which anonymity is defensible, O'Neill concludes that, in general, it is antidemocratic:

> Debate is interactive and consequently has elements of corrigibility. When you don't know where the purported voice on the other side of the debate is coming from, even whether it is one voice, when you don't know whether your remarks are being edited and fed in certain ways into some channels and not others, when you don't know how what you say is being spread around—I think that is really likely to prove utterly destructive of democracy in the end. Also, you don't know what interests are being represented in comments that you can't source. Or who's paying for what. These are very basic matters in considering what the media can contribute to democracy. My perception of it is that anonymity neat and pure is probably something that won't be acceptable, and it certainly won't contribute to democracy.[4]

An even more interesting form of anonymity was made available in Europe in 2014: "The European Court of Justice ruled that an individual's 'right to be forgotten' was so strong that Google and other Internet search companies could be forced to remove links even if the information in question was itself accurate and lawful."[5]

As the ruling makes clear, the right to be forgotten joins other fundamental rights of European Union citizenship. The court's justification for the judicial order examines the effect of a search engine on this right:

> The Court points out in this context that processing of personal data carried out by such an operator enables any internet user, when he makes a search on the basis of an individual's name, to obtain, through the list of results, a structured overview of the information relating to that individual on the internet. The Court observes, furthermore, that this information potentially concerns a vast number of aspects of his private life and that, without the search engine, the information could not have been interconnected or could have been only with great difficulty. Internet users may thereby establish a more or less detailed profile of the person searched against. Furthermore, the effect of the interference with the person's rights is heightened on account of the important role played by the internet and search engines in modern society, which render the information contained in such lists of results ubiquitous. In the light of its potential seriousness, such interference cannot, according to the Court, be justified by merely the economic interest which the operator of the engine has in the data processing.[6]

Oblivion, too, is a silence, if not a secret. For Europeans, at least, oblivion is now among their rights, and through that right, they may attempt to keep secret that which has been public. Perhaps being forgotten is as much secrecy as any of us can hope for today.

V

14 THE FUTURE OF SILENCE

I sit in a coffee shop as I write this. A television ensconced on a corner shelf high up the wall chatters about today's weather, traffic conditions on local roads, and last night's murders. Though still early morning, speakers blare a raucous saxophone solo of dissonant jazz. Cell phones laid on nearly every tabletop beep with text messages every few moments. A bearded man behind the counter is grinding coffee beans into powder; an espresso machine whistles steamed milk into a small pitcher; a refrigerator shudders on and off. Moving from table to table, a young woman clatters dirty cups and saucers into a plastic bin. Behind me, a man on a phone is talking to his lawyer about postponing his court date scheduled for later in the day. Although only March, already the air conditioner is grumbling in the window on the other side of the shop. Someone opens the door, and horns, sirens, a car alarm a block away add to the cacophony of this sanctuary for reading, writing, and quiet conversation.

I pick up a *National Geographic* in the little bookcase where a heater used to be. It's four years old, and the first extended article laments the disruption of marine life in the depths of the ocean because of human noise. I learn that in 2009 the United States Supreme Court found in favor of that noise: "The Court's decision protected the right of naval vessels to test submarine-hunting sonar systems, whose intense sound pulses have been linked to several mass whale strandings. But the Navy is not the lone villain. Oil company ships towing arrays of air guns fire round-the-clock fusillades loud enough to locate oil buried under the seafloor—and also to be heard hundreds of miles away. Undersea construction operations drive piles into the seafloor and blast holes in it with explosives."

I keep reading to the end of the article:

On most days, says Christopher W. Clark, director of the bioacoustics research program at Cornell University, the area over which whales in coastal waters can hear one another shrinks to only 10 to 20 percent of its natural extent.

Clark studies endangered northern right whales, whose habitat includes busy shipping lanes for the port of Boston. In 2007 he and his colleagues deployed a network of seafloor recorders and automated listening buoys in Massachusetts Bay. From three years of continuous recordings, they then compiled a complete underwater "noise budget." Color animations of the data show the calls of right whales getting all but obliterated as ships pass. "The whales' social network is constantly being ripped and reformed," Clark says. Unable to communicate, individual whales have trouble finding each other and spend more time on their own.[1]

I close the magazine and find the theme of the issue shouting in all capital letters at me from the yellow-trimmed cover: "POPULATION 7 BILLION: How your world will change." But I'm still thinking about all those right whales vainly calling out for companionship in the noisy depths of the Atlantic.

So what is the future of silence?

More lonely whales, I fear.

NOTES

Chapter 1

1 "Americans' Belief in God, Miracles and Heaven Decline," Harris Interactive, December 16, 2013. Accessed February 22, 2015. http://www.harrisinteractive.com/NewsRoom/HarrisPolls/tabid/447/ctl/ReadCustom%20Default/mid/1508/ArticleId/1353/Default.aspx.

2 Naftali Bendavid, "Europe's Empty Churches Go on Sale," *The Wall Street Journal*, January 3–4, 2015, A8.

Chapter 2

1 Mark Ellwood, "The Sound of Luxury," *Departures*, September 2014, 190.

2 Jason Cammisa, "America's most fuel-efficient new car isn't a Prius: You'll never believe what beats it," *Road & Track*, February 24, 2014. Accessed February 24, 2015. http://www.roadandtrack.com/go/news/americas-most-fuel-efficient-new-car-is-not-a-toyota-prius?src=rss&dclid=CMaQqqq6tb4CFY3Z5Qod-C8AyA.

3 Dan Neil, "Mercedes-Maybach S600: The Silence Is Deafening," *The Wall Street Journal*, February 7–8, 2015, D11. Accessed February 23, 2015. http://www.wsj.com/articles/mercedes-maybach-s600-the-silence-is-deafening-1423249856?KEYWORDS=rumble+seat.

4 Alex Lockwood, "Why Noise Matters," *Counterfire*, February 2, 2012. Accessed February 24, 2015. http://www.counterfire.org/articles/book-reviews/15488-why-noise-matters.

Chapter 3

1 Conversation with Larry Blake, New Orleans, February 25, 2015.

2 José Ortega y Gasset, *Meditations on Quixote*, trans. Evelyn Rugg and Diego Marín (New York: W. W. Norton & Company, Inc., 1961), 57–58.

3 Rose Eveleth, "Earth's Quietest Place Will Drive You Crazy in 45 Minutes," *Smithsonian.com*, December 17, 2013. Accessed March 23, 2015. http://www.smithsonianmag.com/smart-news/earths-quietest-place-will-drive-you-crazy-in-45-minutes-180948160/?no-ist.

4 Ted Thornhill, "We all crave it, but can you stand the silence?" *Daily Mail*, April 5, 2012. Accessed March 23, 2015. http://www.dailymail.co.uk/sciencetech/article-2124581/The-worlds-quietest-place-chamber-Orfield-Laboratories.html.

5 George Prochnik, *In Pursuit of Silence: Listening for Meaning in a World of Noise* (New York: Anchor Books, 2010), 166.

6 Prochnik, *In Pursuit of Silence*, 4.

7 One Square Inch: A Sanctuary for Silence at Olympic National Park. Accessed March 23, 2015. http://onesquareinch.org/about/.

8 Harold Pinter, *Landscape and Silence* (New York: Grove Press, 1970), 43.

Chapter 4

1 Marc McCutcheon, *Everyday Life in the 1800s* (Cincinnati: Writer's Digest Books, 1993), 168.

2 Michel Foucault, *Discipline & Punish: The Birth of the Prison*, trans. Alan Sheridan (New York: Pantheon, 1977), 237–39.

3 Laura Sullivan, "Timeline: Solitary Confinement in U.S. Prisons," National Public Radio, July 26, 2006, 7:52 ET. Accessed February 22, 2015. http://www.npr.org/templates/story/story.php?storyId=5579901.

4 Peter Scharff Smith, "The Effects of Solitary Confinement on Prison Inmates: A Brief History and Review of the Literature," in *Crime and Justice*, ed. Michael Tonry (Chicago: The University of Chicago Press, vol. 34, no. 1, 2006), 441–528 (460). http://www.jstor.org/stable/10.1086/500626.

5 Smith, "The Effects of Solitary Confinement on Prison Inmates: A Brief History and Review of the Literature," 442–43.

6 Andrew Gumbel, "The Scorched Earth Solution: Solitary Confinement in America," *Los Angeles Review of Books*, October 6, 2013. Accessed March 13, 2015. http://lareviewofbooks.org/essay/the-scorched-earth-solution-solitary-confinement-in-america.

7   Michael Kimmelman, "Prison Architecture and the Question of Ethics," *The New York Times*, February 16, 2015. Accessed February 17, 2015. http://www.nytimes.com/2015/02/17/arts/design/prison-architecture-and-the-question-of-ethics.html?_r=0.

8   Anton Chekhov, "The Bet." Accessed February 22, 2015. http://www.gutenberg.org/cache/epub/13437/pg13437.html.

9   Brian Durant, "The Silence," *The Twilight Zone Vortex*, Wednesday, September 10, 2014. Accessed February 22, 2015. http://twilightzonevortex.blogspot.com/2014/09/the-silence.html.

10 Toby Kamps, "(. . .)," in *Silence*, ed. Toby Kamps and Steve Seid (Houston: Menil Foundation, Inc., 2012), 74.

11 Roberta Smith, "A Year in a Cage: A Life Shrunk to Expand Art," *The New York Times*, February 18, 2009. Accessed February 22, 2015. http://www.nytimes.com/2009/02/19/arts/design/19perf.html?_r=1&.

12 Breon Mitchell, "Kafka and the Hunger Artists," in *Kafka and the Contemporary Critical Performance: Centenary Readings*, ed. Alan Udoff (Bloomington: Indiana University Press, 1987), 236–55.

Chapter 5

1   Diarmaid MacCulloch, *Silence: A Christian History* (New York: Viking, 2013), 76.

2   MacCulloch, *Silence: A Christian History*, 63–64.

3   Ibid., 96–97.

4   George Jonas, *The Happy Hungry Man* (Toronto: House of Anansi, 1970), 9.

Chapter 6

1 Kyle Gann, *No Such Thing as Silence: John Cage's 4'33"* (New Haven: Yale University Press, 2010), 180.

2 "MoMA gets John Cage's silence," November 22, 2012. Accessed February 23, 2015. http://www.phaidon.com/ agenda/art/articles/2012/november/22/moma-gets-john-cages-silence/.

3 Frank Leonard, *4'33" – Brass Quintet Arrangement*. Accessed February 22, 2015. https://www.youtube.com/watch?v=_v46feKoOoI.

4 http://en.wikipedia.org/wiki/Erwin_Schulhoff.

5 Gann, *No Such Thing as Silence: John Cage's 4'33,"* 120.

6 https://www.walden.org/documents/file/Library/About%20 Thoreau/D/Dial/Homer.pdf.

7 Gann, *No Such Thing as Silence: John Cage's 4'33,"* 186.

8 Leah Binkovitz, "The quiet, quiet signs of Rothko Chapel," September 30, 2014, updated November 11, 2014. Accessed February 22, 2015. http://www.houstonchronicle.com/local/ gray-matters/article/The-quiet-quiet-signs-of-Rothko-Chapel-5788978.php#/0.

9 Selden Rodman, *Conversations with Artists* (New York: The Devin-Adair Company, 1957), 93.

10 Jacob Baal-Teshuva, *Rothko* (Cologne: Taschen, 2003), 50.

11 Thomas B. Cole, "The Cover," *Journal of the American Medical Association* (*JAMA*) 305, no. 11 (March 16, 2011): 1066.

Chapter 7

1 Augustine, *The Confessions*, trans. Henry Chadwick (Oxford: Oxford University Press, 1991), 92–93.

2 Roger Chartier, "The Practical Impact of Writing," in *History of Private Life*, vol. 3: *Passions of the Renaissance*, ed. Roger Chartier (Cambridge, MA: Harvard University Press, 1993), 125.

3 Clara Claiborne Park, "The Mother of the Muses: In Praise of Memory," *The American Scholar* 50, no. 1 (1980–81): 55–71 (67).

4 Park, "The Mother of the Muses: In Praise of Memory," 63.

5 Bo Yao et al., "Silent Reading of Direct versus Indirect Speech Activates Voice-selective Areas in the Auditory Cortex," *Journal Of Cognitive Neuroscience* 23, no. 10 (October 2011): 3146–52 (3149–50).

6 Marcela Perrone-Bertolotti et al., "How Silent Is Silent Reading? Intracerebral Evidence for Top-Down Activation of Temporal Voice Areas during Reading," *The Journal of Neuroscience* 32, no. 49, 17554–62 PMID: 23223279, (17554).

7 Betolotti-Perrone, "How Silent Is Silent Reading," 17560.

8 Ibid., 17558.

9 Ibid., 17560.

10 Ibid., 17560.

11 Ibid., 17554.

12 Julie Cross, "Do you hear a voice in your head when you read? If not . . . you could be dyslexic," *Daily Mail*. Updated: 16:00 EST, April 3, 2010. Accessed February 3, 2015. http://www.dailymail.co.uk/health/article-1263307/Do-hear-voice-head-read-If--dyslexic.html.

13 Cross.

Chapter 8

1 Conversation with Michael Cerveris, New Orleans, February 19, 2015.

2 Paul Simon, "Isn't It Rich?" *The New York Times*, October 27, 2010. Accessed March 5, 2015. http://www.nytimes.com/2010/10/31/books/review/Simon-t.html?pagewanted=all

3 Peter Hall, "Directing Pinter," in *Harold Pinter: You Never Heard Such Silence*, ed. Alan Bold (London: Vision Press Limited, 1984), 26.

4 John Biguenet, *Shotgun* (New York: Dramatists Play Service, Inc., 2011), 34–36.

5 http://en.wikipedia.org/wiki/Silence_(1969_play).

6 Leslie Kane, *The Language of Silence: On the Unspoken and the Unspeakable in Modern Drama* (Rutherford: Fairleigh Dickinson University Press, 1984), 27.

7 Maurice Maeterlinck, *Le Trésors des humbles* (Paris: Mercure de France, 1896), 22.

8 Susan Sontag, "The Aesthetics of Silence," *Styles of Radical Will* (New York: Dell, 1978), 5.

9 Lyn Gardner, "Is the Playwright Dead?" *The Guardian*, January 13, 2015. Accessed March 14, 2015. http://www.theguardian.com/stage/theatreblog/2015/jan/13/is-playwright-dead-david-edgar.

Chapter 9

1 Theodor W. Adorno, "Cultural Criticism and Society," *Prisms*, trans. Samuel and Shierry Weber (Cambridge, MA: The MIT Press, 1981), 34.

2 Theodor W. Adorno, *Negative Dialectics*, trans. E. B. Ashton (New York: The Seabury Press, 1973), 362–63.

Chapter 10

1 http://www.geh.org/taschen/htmlsrc10/m197300570002_ful.html.

2 Henri Cartier-Bresson, *The Mind's Eye: Writings on Photography and Photographers*, trans. Diana C. Stoll (New York: Aperture, 1999), 79.

3 Roland Barthes, *Camera Lucida* (New York: Hill and Wang, 1981), 6.

4 Michael Polanyi, "What Is a Painting?" *The American Scholar* 39 (Autumn 1970): 664.

5 Barthes, *Camera Lucida*, 5–6.

6 Beaumont Newhall, *The History of Photography*, rev. ed. (New York: The Museum of Modern Art, 1964), 71.

Chapter 11

1 Rainer Maria Rilke, "Some Reflections on Dolls," in *Where Silence Reigns: Selected Prose*, trans. G. Craig Houston (New York: New Directions, 1978), 46–47.

2 E. T. A. Hoffmann, "The Sandman," in *Selected Writings of E. T. A. Hoffmann*, vol. 1, ed. and trans. Leonard J. Kent and Elizabeth C. Knight (Chicago: The University of Chicago Press, 1969), 156.

3   Sigmund Freud, *The Uncanny*, trans. David McLintock (Harmondsworth: Penguin, 2003), 147–48.

4   Freud, *The Uncanny*, 159.

5   Hoffmann, "The Sandman," 161.

6   Ibid., 162.

7   Ibid., 154.

8   Ibid., 158.

9   Ibid., 163.

10 Walter Benjamin, "Old Toys: The Toy Exhibition at the Märkisches Museum," in *On Dolls* (Kindle Locations 1059–1071). Notting Hill Editions; Kindle Edition. (2012-11-20).

11 Marina Warner, "On the Threshold: Sleeping Beauties," *Phantasmagoria: Spirit Visions, Metaphors, and Media into the Twenty-first Century* (Oxford: Oxford University Press, 2006); *On Dolls* (Kindle Locations 1235–1241). Notting Hill Editions; Kindle Edition. (2012-11-20).

12 http://en.wikipedia.org/wiki/Marie_Tussaud.

13 Warner, "On the Threshold: Sleeping Beauties," Kindle Locations 1457–1458.

14 Bruno Schulz, "Tailors' Dummies," in *The Street of Crocodiles*, trans. Celina Wieniewska (Harmondsworth: Penguin, 1977), 65.

15 L. Frank Baum, *Ozma of Oz*, in *The Wizard of Oz: The First Five Novels* (New York: Fall River Press, 2013), 325–26.

16 Charles Baudelaire, "Morale du Joujou" first appeared in *Le Monde littéraire*, April 17, 1853, and was included in *L'Art romantique* (1869), translation by Paul Keegan, from *Essays on Dolls*, ed. Idris Parry (Harmondsworth: Penguin, 1994); *On Dolls* (Kindle Locations 345–353). Notting Hill Editions; Kindle Edition. (2012-11-20).

17 Hans Bellmer, quoted in Peter Webb and Robert Short, *Hans Bellmer* (New York: Quartet Books, 1985), 29.

18 Robert Hughes, *The Shock of the New* (New York: Knopf, 1981), 252.

Chapter 12

1 Bessie Dendrinos and Emilia Ribeiro Pedro, "Giving Street Directions: The Silent Role of Women," in *Silence: Interdisciplinary Perspectives*, ed. Adam Jaworski (Berlin: Mouton de Gruyter, 1997), 215–38. All related quotes are from this source.

2 http://evene.lefigaro.fr/citation/rien-rehausse-autorite-mieux-silence-splendeur-forts-refuge-fai-41364.php.

3 http://www.goodreads.com/author/show/490153.Charles_de_Gaulle.

4 http://www.quotationspage.com/quote/30170.html.

5 http://www.goodreads.com/author/quotes/13560.Leonardo_da_Vinci.

Chapter 13

1 *Silence: A Thirteenth-Century French Romance*, trans. Sarah Roche-Mahdi (East Lansing: Michigan State University Press, 2007), xi–xii.

2 Jenny Nordberg, "Afghan Boys Are Prized, So Girls Live the Part," *The New York Times*, A1, September 20, 2010. Accessed

March 21, 2015. http://www.nytimes.com/2010/09/21/world/asia/21gender.html.

3 John Thornhill, "How can we defeat terrorism if all the trust has gone?" *Financial Times*, August 23, 2013.

4 Josh Booth, "Power and publication: an interview with Onora O'Neill," *King's Review*, October 28, 2013. Accessed March 22, 2015. http://kingsreview.co.uk/magazine/blog/2013/10/28/power-and-publication-an-interview-with-onora-oneill/.

5 Editorial Board, "Ordering Google to Forget," *The New York Times*, May 13, 2014. Accessed March 22, 2015. http://www.nytimes.com/2014/05/14/opinion/ordering-google-to-forget.html.

6 Court of Justice of the European Union, "Judgment in Case C-131/12: Google Spain SL, Google Inc. v Agencia Española de Protección de Datos, Mario Costeja González," Luxembourg: Press Release No. 70/14, May 13, 2014. Accessed March 21, 2015. http://curia.europa.eu/jcms/upload/docs/application/pdf/2014-05/cp140070en.pdf.

Chapter 14

1 Leslie Allen, "Drifting in Static," *National Geographic* 219, no. 1 (January 2011): 33.

BIBLIOGRAPHY

Adorno, Theodor W. "Cultural Criticism and Society." *Prisms*. Cambridge, MA: The MIT Press, 1981, 17–34 .

Adorno, Theodor W. *Negative Dialectics*. New York: The Seabury Press, 1973.

Allen, Leslie. "Drifting in Static." *National Geographic* 219, no. 1 (January 2011): 33.

Augustine. *The Confessions*. Translated by Henry Chadwick, 92–93. Oxford: Oxford University Press, 1991.

Baal-Teshuva, Jacob. *Rothko*. Cologne: Taschen, 2003.

Barthes, Roland. *Camera Lucida*. New York: Hill and Wang, 1981.

Baudelaire, Charles. "Morale du Joujou" first appeared in *Le Monde littéraire*, 17 April 1853, and was included in *L'Art romantique* (1869); Translation by Paul Keegan, from *Essays on Dolls*, edited by Idris Parry. Harmondsworth: Penguin, 1994; *On Dolls* (Kindle Locations 345–353). Notting Hill Editions; Kindle Edition. (2012-11-20).

Baum, L. Frank. *Ozma of Oz* in *The Wizard of Oz: The First Five Novels*. New York: Fall River Press, 2013.

Bellmer, Hans, quoted in Peter Webb and Robert Short. *Hans Bellmer*. New York: Quartet Books, 1985, 29.

Benjamin, Walter. "Old Toys: The Toy Exhibition at the Märkisches Museum." In *On Dolls* (Kindle Locations 1059–1071). Notting Hill Editions; Kindle Edition. (2012-11-20).

Biguenet, John. *Shotgun*. New York: Dramatists Play Service, Inc., 2011.

Booth, Josh. "Power and publication: an interview with Onora O'Neill." *King's Review*, October 28, 2013. Accessed March 22, 2015. http://kingsreview.co.uk/magazine/blog/2013/10/28/power-and-publication-an-interview-with-onora-oneill/.

Cage, John. *Notations*. New York: Something Else Press, Inc. 1969.

Cammisa, Jason. "America's most fuel-efficient new car isn't a Prius: You'll never believe what beats it." *Road & Track,* February 24, 2014. Accessed February 25, 2015. http://www.roadandtrack.com/go/news/americas-most-fuel-efficient-new-car-is-not-a-toyota-prius?src=rss&dclid=CMaQqqq6tb4CFY3Z5Qod-C8AyA.

Cartier-Bresson, Henri. *The Mind's Eye: Writings on Photography and Photographers*. Translated by Diana C. Stoll. New York: Aperture, 1999.

Chartier, Roger. "The Practical Impact of Writing." In *History of Private Life*, vol. 3: *Passions of the Renaissance*, ed. Robert Chartier, 111–59. Cambridge, MA: Harvard University Press, 1993.

Chekhov, Anton. "The Bet." Accessed February 22, 2015. http://www.gutenberg.org/cache/epub/13437/pg13437.html.

Court of Justice of the European Union. "Judgment in Case C-131/12: Google Spain SL, Google Inc. v Agencia Española de Protección de Datos, Mario Costeja González." Luxembourg: Press Release No. 70/14, May 13, 2014. Accessed March 21, 2015. http://curia.europa.eu/jcms/upload/docs/application/pdf/2014-05/cp140070en.pdf

Cross, Julie. "Do you hear a voice in your head when you read? If not . . . you could be dyslexic." *Daily Mail*. Updated: 16:00 EST, April 3, 2010. Accessed February 3, 2015. http://www.dailymail.co.uk/health/article-1263307/Do-hear-voice-head-read-If--dyslexic.html.

Dendrinos, Bessie, and Emilia Ribeiro Pedro. "Giving Street Directions: The Silent Role of Women." In *Silence: Interdisciplinary Perspectives*, edited by Adam Jaworski, 215–38. Berlin: Mouton de Gruyter, 1997.

Durant, Brian. "The Silence." *The Twilight Zone Vortex*, Wednesday, September 10, 2014. Accessed February 22, 2015. http://twilightzonevortex.blogspot.com/2014/09/the-silence.html.

Ellwood, Mark. "The Sound of Luxury." *Departures*, September 2014, 190.

Eveleth, Rose. "Earth's Quietest Place Will Drive You Crazy in 45 Minutes." *Smithsonian.com*, December 17, 2013. Accessed March 23, 2015. http://www.smithsonianmag.com/smart-news/earths-quietest-place-will-drive-you-crazy-in-45-minutes-180948160/?no-ist.

Foucault, Michel. *Discipline & Punish: The Birth of the Prison*. Translated by Alan Sheridan. New York: Pantheon, 1977.

Freud, Sigmund. *The Uncanny*. Translated by David McLintock. Harmondsworth: Penguin, 2003.

Gann, Kyle. *No Such Thing as Silence: John Cage's 4'33"*. New Haven: Yale University Press, 2010.

Gardner, Lyn. "Is the Playwright Dead?" *The Guardian*, January 13, 2015. Accessed March 14, 2015. http://www.theguardian.com/stage/theatreblog/2015/jan/13/is-playwright-dead-david-edgar.

Gumbel, Andrew. "The Scorched Earth Solution: Solitary Confinement in America." *Los Angeles Review of Books*, October 6, 2013. Accessed March 13, 2015. http://lareviewofbooks.org/essay/the-scorched-earth-solution-solitary-confinement-in-america.

Hall, Peter. "Directing Pinter." In *Harold Pinter: You Never Heard Such Silence*, edited by Alan Bold, 26. London: Vision Press Limited, 1984.

Hoffmann, E. T. A. "The Sandman." In *Selected Writings of E. T. A. Hoffmann*, vol. 1, edited and translated by Leonard J. Kent and Elizabeth C. Knight. Chicago: The University of Chicago Press, 1969, 137–67.

Hughes, Robert. *The Shock of the New*. New York: Knopf, 1981.

Jaworski, Adam, ed. *Silence: Interdisciplinary Perspectives*. Berlin: Mouton de Gruyter, 1997.

Jonas, George. *The Happy Hungry Man*. Toronto: House of Anansi, 1970.

Kamps, Toby, and Steve Seid. *Silence*. Houston: Menil Foundation, Inc., 2012.

Kane, Leslie. *The Language of Silence: On the Unspoken and the Unspeakable in Modern Drama*. Rutherford: Fairleigh Dickinson University Press, 1984.

Kimmelman, Michael. "Prison Architecture and the Question of Ethics." *The New York Times*, February 16, 2015. Accessed February 17, 2015. http://www.nytimes.com/2015/02/17/arts/design/prison-architecture-and-the-question-of-ethics.html?_r=0.

Lockwood, Alex. "Why Noise Matters." *Counterfire*, February 2, 2012. Accessed February 24, 2015. http://www.counterfire.org/articles/book-reviews/15488-why-noise-matters.

MacCulloch, Diarmaid. *Silence: A Christian History*. New York: Viking, 2013.

Maeterlinck, Maurice. *Le Trésors des humbles*. Paris: Mercure de France, 1896.

McCutcheon, Marc. *Everyday Life in the 1800s*. Cincinnati: Writer's Digest Books, 1993.

Mitchell, Breon. "Kafka and the Hunger Artists." In *Kafka and the Contemporary Critical Performance: Centenary Readings*, edited by Alan Udoff, 236–55. Bloomington: Indiana University Press, 1987.

Neil, Dan. "Mercedes-Maybach S600: The Silence Is Deafening." *The Wall Street Journal*, D11, February 7–8, 2015. Accessed February 23, 2015. http://www.wsj.com/articles/mercedes-maybach-s600-the-silence-is-deafening-1423249856?KEYWORDS=rumble+seat.

Newhall, Beaumont. *The History of Photography*, rev. ed. New York: The Museum of Modern Art, 1964.

Nordberg, Jenny. "Afghan Boys Are Prized, So Girls Live the Part." *The New York Times*, A1, September 20, 2010. Accessed March 21, 2015. http://www.nytimes.com/2010/09/21/world/asia/21gender.html.

One Square Inch: A Sanctuary for Silence at Olympic National Park. Accessed March 23, 2015. http://onesquareinch.org/about/.

Ortega y Gasset, José. *Meditations on Quixote*. Translated by Evelyn Rugg and Diego Marín. New York: W. W. Norton & Company, Inc., 1961.

Park, Clara Claiborne. "The Mother of the Muses: In Praise of Memory." *The American Scholar* 50, no. 1 (1980–81): 55–71.

Parry, Idris, ed. *Essays on Dolls*. Harmondsworth: Penguin, 1994.

Perrone-Bertolotti, M., J. Kujala, J. R. Vidal, C. M. Hamame, T. Ossandon, O. Bertrand, L. Minotti, P. Kahane, K. Jerbi, and J. P. Lachaux. "How Silent Is Silent Reading? Intracerebral Evidence for Top-Down Activation of Temporal Voice Areas during Reading." *The Journal of Neuroscience* 32, no. 49, 17554-17562 PMID: 23223279.

Pinter, Harold. http://en.wikipedia.org/wiki/Silence_(1969_play).

Pinter, Harold. *Landscape and Silence*. New York: Grove Press, 1970.

Polanyi, Michael. "What Is a Painting?" *The American Scholar* 39 (Autumn 1970): 664.

Prochnik, George. *In Pursuit of Silence: Listening for Meaning in a World of Noise*. New York: Anchor Books, 2010.

Rilke, Rainer Maria. "Some Reflections on Dolls." In *Where Silence Reigns: Selected Prose*, Translated by G. Craig Houston, 43–50. New York: New Directions, 1978.

Rodman, Selden. *Conversations with Artists*. New York: The Devin-Adair Company, 1957.

Schulz, Bruno. "Tailors' Dummies." In *The Street of Crocodiles*, translated by Celina Wieniewska. Harmondsworth: Penguin, 1977, 51–71.

Silence: A Thirteenth-Century French Romance. Translated by Sarah Roche-Mahdi, xi–xii. East Lansing: Michigan State University Press, 2007.

Simon, Paul. "Isn't It Rich?" *The New York Times*, October 27, 2010. http://www.nytimes.com/2010/10/31/books/review/Simon-t.html?pagewanted=all.

Smith, Peter Scharff. "The Effects of Solitary Confinement on Prison Inmates: A Brief History and Review of the Literature." In *Crime and Justice*, vol. 34, no. 1. Chicago: The University of Chicago Press, 2006. http://www.jstor.org/stable/10.1086/500626.

Smith, Roberta. "A Year in a Cage: A Life Shrunk to Expand Art." *The New York Times*, February 18, 2009. Accessed February 22, 2015. http://www.nytimes.com/2009/02/19/arts/design/19perf.html?_r=1&.

Sontag, Susan. "The Aesthetics of Silence." In *Styles of Radical Will.* New York: Dell, 1978.

Sullivan, Laura. "Timeline: Solitary Confinement in U.S. Prisons." National Public Radio. Accessed February 22, 2015. http://www.npr.org/templates/story/story.php?storyId=5579901.

Thornhill, John. "How can we defeat terrorism if all the trust has gone?" *Financial Times*, August 23, 2013.

Thornhill, Ted. "We all crave it, but can you stand the silence?" *Daily Mail*, April 5, 2012. Accessed March 23, 2015. http://www.dailymail.co.uk/sciencetech/article-2124581/The-worlds-quietest-place-chamber-Orfield-Laboratories.html.

Warner, Marina. "On the Threshold: Sleeping Beauties." *Phantasmagoria: Spirit Visions, Metaphors, and Media into the Twenty-first Century.* Oxford: Oxford University Press, 2006; *On Dolls* (Kindle Locations 1235–1241 and 1457–1458). Notting Hill Editions; Kindle Edition. (2012-11-20).

Webb, Peter, and Robert Short. *Hans Bellmer.* New York: Quartet Books, 1985.

Yao, B., P. Belin, and C. Scheepers. "Silent Reading of Direct versus Indirect Speech Activates Voice-selective Areas in the Auditory Cortex." *Journal Of Cognitive Neuroscience* 23, no. 10 (October 2011): 3146–52.

Yao, B., P. Belin, and C. Scheepers. "Brain 'talks over' boring quotes: top-down activation of voice-selective areas while listening to monotonous direct speech quotations." *NeuroImage: A Journal of Brain Function* 60, no. 3 (April 2012): 1832–42. doi: 10.1016/j.neuroimage.2012.01.111; Epub 2012 Jan 28.

INDEX